TOD

DISCIPLINE

Step-by-step Guide to Raising Responsible and Curious Children

(Effective Strategy to Empathically Discipline Your Toddlers)

Larry Tipton

Published by Jennifer Windy

Larry Tipton

Toddler Discipline: Step-by-step Guide to Raising Responsible and Curious Children (Effective Strategy to Empathically Discipline Your Toddlers)

ISBN 978-1-989965-73-3

Legal & Disclaimer

The information contained in this book is not designed to replace or take the place of any form of medicine or professional medical advice. The information in this book has been provided for educational and entertainment purposes only.

The information contained in this book has been compiled from sources deemed reliable, and it is accurate to the best of the Author's knowledge; however, the Author cannot guarantee its accuracy and validity and cannot be held liable for any errors or omissions. Changes are periodically made to this book. You must consult your doctor or get professional medical advice before using any of the suggested remedies, techniques, or information in this book.

Upon using the information contained in this book, you agree to hold harmless the Author from and against any damages, costs, and expenses, including any legal fees potentially resulting from the application of any of the information provided by this guide. This disclaimer applies to any damages or injury caused by the use and application, whether directly or indirectly, of any advice or information presented, whether for breach of contract, tort, negligence, personal injury, criminal intent, or under any other cause of action.

You agree to accept all risks of using the information presented inside this book. You need to consult a professional medical practitioner in order to ensure you are both able and healthy enough to participate in this program.

Table of Contents

Introduction

Among the most questions parents ask are topics associated with separation anxiety, behavior problems, raising your children with the positive discipline, overcoming tantrums and challenges, building positive relationships, and teaching respect and responsibility.

When our babies turn toddlers, parenting changes dramatically, they have constant attention, and they have to be watched in the least times because they're so interested in everything. If you are not watching them, you're going to find yourself in trouble. Simple as that, they will be clever in some very destructive ways.

When your child reaches the top of 2-3 years old, the character of their true personality will begin to shine. Not that it's not always present, just that it becomes more prevalent, more defined, this may become more noticeable, day by day. It should be encouraged and nurtured for positive thought and developments to create confidence.

Providing positive first-time experiences with things will endear the mind confidently in proceeding with its natural curiosities. This process will multiply in dimensions beyond our reasoning. Building a connection by encouraging open communication about everything. Celebrate talks about everything and anything, try to include some details of how they feel about things if the kid is pretending to accompany for touch while. Then, subtly cause the direction to vary by your influence and steer it from there.

Allow your child the power to act out some fantasies (healthy ones) and provides props and take part in the fun. Play superman, or king of the mountain games, to bond and connect with your child during these times of play attempt to inject the maximum amount of learning possible. During this period, the brain can take a vast amount of learning skills with many rooms to spare.

Incorporate learning skills into everyday activities within the lifetime of the kid during these years and on. Your child's brain is far sort of a sponge at that point, and you'll want them to take in all they will. Toddler parenting is often fun but is additionally a serious challenge, thanks to how constant the care must be administered. It is often hard to stay up, especially when other considerations can inherit play.

Toddlers also tend to attempt to push the bounds of our patients to the boundaries. they're simply learning the limit to their power and beyond, which will pull the chains of command; this is often also vital in our parenting process. it's important to surround these years with comfortable, safe feelings of expression; it is often that confidence can build alongside the positive impressions. The more the positive experiences fill the brain, the more confidence will build and develop problem-solving naturally.

Toddlers are often great fun and their inquisitive nature will undoubtedly one among the steepest learning curves, both the kid and you'll ever face, but when your toddler is prying into something which could lead on to them becoming hurt or hurting someone or something else, you would like to require the reins and apply toddler discipline.

And being the parent of a toddler are often exciting, exhilarating, and exhausting - all at once! Your biddable baby has now become a moving, grooving tot with attitude, and every one the changes that this entails are often confusing to you and your child, you're faced with issues like discipline (what happens when your child discovers that 'no' is the most powerful word in his vocabulary?), eating (does spaghetti sauce count as a vegetable?), learning, teaching social skills, and trying to urge enough sleep to stay up together with your little dynamo.

Non-compliance, aggression, and destructiveness are common misbehaviors among toddlers and pre-school children, and a few young children exhibit these behaviors at very high rates. These, especially hard-to-manage children, are in danger of developing serious externalizing disorders and may cause considerable distress for them.

Parental discipline is assumed to contribute to the event and maintenance of such misbehavior. Specifically, discipline that's characterized as either lax, permissive, and inconsistent or as overreactive, authoritarian, and coercive has been repeatedly linked with the presence of children's behavior problems. Furthermore, when parents are taught to use more consistent, moderate, and firm discipline strategies, their children exhibit significantly fewer behavior problems.

Words like hurry and tidy are meaningless to a toddler, yet, we sleep in a fast-paced world that demands such a lot from us that frustration is often the order of most days: we are bombarded by pressure to be perfect a parent - to possess a well-behaved child who will comply as we educate him from one education to another lest he fails to realize his academic potential when he reaches school age.

When our tasks mount, it is often very tempting to easily pop on a DVD, especially if the manufacturers claim it'll make your child smarter. On the other hand, taking the straightforward way is certain to fire up guilty feelings that you simply could also be letting your child down if you are not an all-dancing, all-gluing entertainment coordinator.

Relax! Toddler Discipline will assist you in banishing your performance anxiety and finding the 'terrific' in your toddler. This guide offers an easy, fuss-free approach to instilling discipline during this magical stage of development.

As the name suggests, Toddler Discipline is full of practical strategies that you simply can use immediately to beat the inevitable challenges of living with a touch one that is discovering the planet and the way it revolves around him (or not). This parenting guide will show you ways to boost your children with positive discipline, overcome tantrums and challenges, and teach your children respect and responsibility.

Overall, Toddler Discipline will show how you'll unleash your child's natural potential to be happy, bright, and friendly without too many tears and tantrums (for you or your child!). Also, as offering practical strategies to encourage optimal development and cooperation without thwarting your child's innate spirit and sense of discovery, toddler tactics encourages you to be kind to yourself as you share this amazing journey with your child.

Chapter 1: Understanding And Working With Your Toddler's Psychology... And Why!

There is a reason why it has become culturally accepted to view our tiny toddlers as almost an entirely different class of people, and sometimes even as an entirely different species! This is tongue in cheek, of course, but there are many reasons for why it can be so difficult for parents and caregivers to understand their tiny toddler's behavior, especially at the stage commonly referred to as the Terrible Twos! Babies come into this world entirely dependent on their parents and caregivers, and we are physically able to control most aspects of their lives in those very early days. As our babies become more mobile, this becomes more and more difficult to do, and once the toddler years hit, this newfound mobility is tied to a cognitive leap that inspires our little one's to assert this newfound independence in ways that can be very trying for the adults around them!

Infant Guidance

To better understand how loving and respectful discipline works for our toddlers, let's first look at the role of loving and respectful discipline that begins as soon as our babies enter into this world. As we touched on in the introduction, discipline does not equal punishment. When we refer to discipline for newborns, we are certainly not referring to or condoning any sort of physical punishment that uses pain or discomfort to enforce a behavioral guideline. We are instead referring to discipline in its positive association, as a tool to teach and guide. While the newborn stage may not seem like the age that we are doing much beyond around the clock direct care (feeding, changing diapers, bathing, etc.) our responsive care and attention **is** teaching and guiding our little ones towards an important lesson. We are teaching them that they can count on us, and we are there for them. Discipline can be and is as simple as that.

In that first year of life, our tiny, precious babies are learning what to expect of the world and what relationships look like. What they learn from their parents and caregivers in these very early days will set the stage for the development of their sense of self and their self-esteem as they continue to develop. When we are responsive to our baby's cries and physical cues and meet their needs efficiently, lovingly, and respectfully, we are teaching them that they are cared for, supported, and worthy of attention and love. These are considered to be the fundamental building blocks of a healthy sense of self and self-esteem.

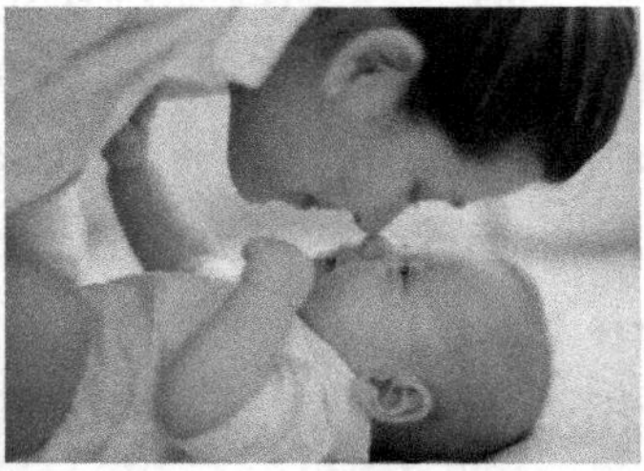

It can be a common fear of some parents and caregivers they might “spoil” their baby by meeting their every cry and their every cue, but the American Academy of Pediatrics- the United State’s foremost authority on child health and development- states that this is simply not the case. You have a baby, not a perishable food item- there is no such thing as a spoiled baby! They even go on to assert that research shows that the more responsive we are to these very early needs in infancy, the less likely our little ones are to need extra reassurance as they enter the toddler years. This early foundation of trust is very important to our future toddler's mental, emotional, and psychological health.

Leaps and Bounds

The one-year mark is what is widely considered to be when your child hits the toddler years. There is so much happening in our little one's world at this age, isn't there? Most children are taking their first steps around this time, and their vocabulary is growing in leaps and bounds. Some days it may even seem like our little one is growing and learning in their sleep, as they often seem to master new skills and abilities almost overnight. Their brains are like little sponges in these early toddler days, and they keep parents and caregivers on their toes with their curiosity and newfound independence. While it is impressive to see our little ones as they grow and develop so quickly, there is somewhat of a drawback to this. These huge leaps may lead us to believe that our little ones are capable of more than they may actually be capable of, developmentally.

This is where understanding our toddler's psychology comes into play. There are so many developmental leaps that our toddlers are making in the years between ages 1-3. Just imagine what must be taking place under the surface as our toddler goes from taking their first halting and unsteady steps as a wobbly one-year-old to when they are scaling playground equipment by themselves to go down the slide at the neighborhood park just a few short months later!

These toddler transformations are exactly the sorts of significant physical leaps and milestones that are prevalent in the toddler years, including the easily visible ones such as learning to use their bodies to walk, run, and jump.

Fine motor skills, such as the ability to pick up tiny objects such as pebbles or Lego pieces are developing. These are the skills that toddlers will need to be able to do everyday tasks such as brushing their teeth, buttoning up their jacket, holding silverware properly, holding and using a pencil, etc. They are any movement that requires use and coordination of the small muscles in the hands.

Gross motor skills, such as the ability to throw a ball, are developing. Their little bodies must learn how to do everything in these early years: they must learn how to climb stairs, how to open doors, how to dress themselves. Gross motor skills are the skills that involve movement of the whole body and require a core strength, such as when balancing on one foot while putting the other into a shoe. Both strength and coordination are developing quickly in these early toddler years.

Toddlers are developing quickly on the cognitive level, too. Their ability to learn and partake in social customs, such as waving hello and goodbye, saying "sorry," when they've done something wrong, and to begin to learn their colors, numbers, letters, nursery rhymes, etc. is all taking place at break-neck speed, especially if we were to compare it to the rates of learning that most adults are typically working at!

Social and emotional skills are the skills that our toddlers need to be able to successfully navigate social situations such as school, work and life. These are the skills that will help our children develop their friendships, manage conflict resolution, manage and handle stress, learn how to make sound decisions and use good judgement, and to develop empathy skills. Parents and caregivers provide the primary model here for these skills, and just as our responsive care in infancy helps to set the foundation for a strong and healthy sense of self and self-esteem, parents and caregivers must also model the social and emotional skills that we want our toddlers to have.

It is unrealistic for parents and caregivers to expect for a two-year-old child to control and manage their own emotions without having a temper tantrum if they watch their parents and their caregivers act out in emotional distress by yelling and slamming doors. Again, our sweet little toddlers are very monkey see, monkey do. Developing emotional regulation is a long process for most toddlers.

Respectful Expectation

As our toddlers are experiencing this expedited rate of physical, developmental, cognitive, social, and emotional growth, it is only natural that some of this may be unsettling for both them and their parents and caregivers. From their limited perspective, the world is so wide and so wondrous. It is also full of so many intriguing things to do, see, and touch, and they often spend most of their days hearing the word "no" as they reach out to explore! From their viewpoint, they only know that the dog's bowl of water on the floor is wet, and they remember that they enjoy exploring wet things and are encouraged to explore water in the bathtub or in the kiddie pool in the backyard, so why not this convenient water source right here in the house? Yet, perplexingly, every time they go near it, they hear "no!" and are moved away from it.

Or perhaps they find themselves watching their parents and caregivers spend their days touching, looking at, and interacting with this portable object that they carry around with them from room to room and place to place, but when their little toddler hands reach out to touch it, they are told "no!" when all they want to do is explore this intriguing object just as they see their primary models do. They don't understand that the smart phone has been placed on the charger and needs to be left alone. All the toddler knows is that this thing that gets a lot of attention and use from everyone else is now finally within their reach, and they'd like to check it out too!

This leads us to one of the major aspects that parents and caregivers must understand about toddlers and their psychology. They are learning how to be and who to be in this world, primarily from looking to see what others do. As parents and caregivers, it can be easy to become preoccupied with ensuring we say the right things to our children, and impart the right wisdom to them at different parts of their lives, but this is not how toddlers learn best. Toddlers will not learn that they should not play in the dog's water bowl after hearing a lengthy explanation about how that is the dog's drinking water, and that splashing in it will make a mess that will then need to be cleaned up. Toddler's will not understand that the phone must be left alone to charge and is not for them after hearing their parents/caregiver's long lecture to leave it alone because otherwise the phone will die and then some important communication may be missed. We need to better recognize where our toddlers are coming from, because our toddlers are not operating from a place where they have the cognitive understanding and the impulse control necessary to understand and act accordingly. In this, it is up to us to structure our world to better accommodate them where they are at.

Toddlers' brains are still in the development phase and it is simply unrealistic to expect our toddlers to be able to fulfill certain behavioral expectations that they are not yet equipped with the proper tools yet to do so. We are referring here specifically to the pre-frontal cortex, which is that part of the brain that is responsible for impulse control and the ability to make sound decisions and control our emotions. Once we recognize that our toddlers are simply not fully equipped with the tools required to meet these expectations, we can then make the shift away from these unrealistic expectations that only cause parents, caregivers, and the toddlers themselves strife. Consider this: Our toddlers do not want to be in the position of making their parents and caregivers unhappy with them, but it can often be that it is our expectations that play a large role in setting them up for this failure of sorts.

It can also be helpful to recognize that the only means our toddlers have to explore and learn about the world around them is through direct manipulation and experimentation, and this is hands on. Their learning is tactile. They have to use their hands to touch and their eyes to inspect. They have to use their nose to smell and yes, even their mouth to taste! (All toddler parents and caregivers are unfortunately all too well acquainted with that particular mode of exploration!) This hands-on experimentation is the only way our toddlers can access and learn about their worlds. If we think about it for a moment, they are not able to pick up their smart phones and do a quick internet search to learn about something that interests them, or run to their local library and ask a librarian for help in finding information on a topic. Picking up an object and giving it a quick taste may be the best they can do with certain things!

What's more, is that our toddlers are in a position of having to learn everything from the bottom up. They are new in this world, and it is big, confusing, and full of people telling them what to do and how to do it. Take a brief moment to truly consider what it is like for a toddler child: They are put down to sleep when they may not actually be sleepy yet, in a bed that has bars and is set up specifically to contain them and keep them in. If they wake in the middle of the night, there is no ability to reach for a drink of water or go grab a late-night snack by themselves, they must cry and yell until someone else comes to their aid. Then once morning arrives, they are still stuck in their bed and must do the same, yelling and crying until someone comes to them. Even once they are pulled out of their crib, their day has been planned for them. They are dressed in clothes they didn't pick out, they are subjected to hygiene rituals they can't do and likely don't completely understand the reason for them, they are fed foods they didn't choose and prepare, and then they are placed in situations they didn't choose, either strapped in a car seat and taken somewhere or set down in a room full of interesting objects such as electronic cords or curtains that they are then told "no!" about when they try to explore them.

Their days continue on like this, very little freedom and autonomy and a “no” at every turn. Can you imagine how frustrating this must be for them, especially as they are going through so many developmental leaps and learning and developing new skills and abilities every day?

Parents and caregivers must first evaluate their expectations as the first step. Are they expecting something that is beyond their toddler’s ability level? Think back to the example of the water dish on the floor. Evaluating this scenario against the knowledge that not only are toddlers essentially hard-wired to learn about the world around them by directly exploring, but that part of their brain that is necessary for them to check this desire to explore against the ongoing direction of “no” is not even fully developed yet. It is necessary to adjust expectations.

Rather than expect that a toddler will be able to curb their self-impulses and desire to explore the dog's water dish, recognize that this is a monumental task for them that borders on the impossible, and instead, remove the toddler's access to the dog's water dish.

We spoke earlier about all of the "no" that our toddlers hear day in, and day out, as they seek to explore and learn about the world in the only way they know how. All of these "no's" contribute to a feeling of frustration and irritation for both the parents, caregivers, and toddlers. A way to easily alleviate this frustration and irritation is to avoid it in the first place. An easy way to do this is to give your toddler the opposite of "no." Give them a space that is only "yes," where they are allowed to touch and explore everything in it. For some people, this space may be a gated off room full of toys, manipulatives, and anything that is toddler safe and friendly, and for others this may just be a toddler playpen area in a living room that is full of toys, manipulatives, and anything that is toddler safe and friendly. It should go without saying that any space that is devoted to yes will need to be as childproofed as possible, because the entire point is to give them a space where they can safely play and explore without hearing the dreaded “no.” This means no bookcases that can be climbed on and pulled over, no end tables with a lamp on it that can be pulled down, no houseplants on a side table that could be knocked over, nothing at all that the toddler will be told “no” about if they pick it up.

This opposite of the “no” space gives both toddlers and their parents and caregivers relief and freedom. Just as much as a toddler grows tired and frustrated of being thwarted with that dastardly “no,” parents and caregivers can quickly tire of having to chase after the curious and explorative toddler and redirect and manage them time and time again. This safe space that gives the toddler freedom and space to explore, learn, and play is called the “yes space" by RIE philosophy proponents. RIE philosophy is a infant/child philosophy that emphasizes respect in parent/caregiver relationships with infants, toddlers, and beyond. This "yes space" is very important in building this respectful relationship, as just as badly as our toddlers want to explore and learn about their world, they also want to do well. They don't want to be chastised and lectured to repeatedly, they want to succeed! Setting up a "yes space" is an important part of setting our toddlers up for success.

Setting up safe spaces for toddlers in the home is important, but what about when we need to take them out with us? If a parent or caregiver needs to run errands, such as heading to the grocery store and then swinging by the post office, what should they expect their toddler to be capable of behaviorally and psychologically? Well, it can be helpful to first consider that for most of us adults, trips to the grocery store and the post office aren't necessarily what we consider to be the definition of a "good time," so perhaps its not so very different for our toddler- except they will have very little tasks to do on these trips and will instead only be along for the ride!

There are essentially two basic schools of thought on taking our toddlers along with us to run errands. One says that it is healthy for our toddlers to accompany their parents and caregivers on tasks such as visits to the grocery store and post office, so they can have the opportunity to learn and practice appropriate behavior in these spaces. The other says that it is disrespectful to our toddlers and unrealistic for parents and caregivers to expect that toddler's will be able to meet our expectations on errands such as these.

Both of these schools of thought are operating on the model of wanting to set our toddlers up for success, aren't they? For the first, the idea is sound that our toddlers will never learn how to behave in these sorts of scenarios if they aren't given opportunities to learn and practice meeting our expectations. Their primary mode of learning comes from observation of their parents and caregivers as they navigate through the world, and so how will a toddler come to learn appropriate behavior in the grocery store or standing in line at the post office, if they never get to see what that looks like?

For many parents and caregivers, this is not even a choice they are able to make, as it is simply necessity to take their toddler along with them to run errands. A way to set up the trip for success is to begin by adjusting our expectations. A two-year-old is not going to find it easy to stand in a long line, creeping at a snail's pace, at the post office. There are things that parents and caregivers can do to help, such as bringing a small toy and/or snack for the toddler to engage with after the excitement of the new place they are in has faded, and to recognize and realize that in a scenario such as a post office, there may be some physical restraint needed to keep their toddler from running around the room. Some parents and caregivers opt to use carriers that allow them to strap their toddler on their front or back, or strollers, so they can be safely restrained and the parent and/or caregiver can still take care of what they came to take care of. Most toddlers enjoy these options greatly as it gives them a safe and secure location to observe and take in their new surroundings, and it gives them the structure and boundary that they need to keep from running around and getting in trouble. Again, we have to remember as parents and caregivers that our toddlers want to succeed, too!

For parents and caregivers that opt not to take their toddlers along on errands that involve putting them in scenarios in which they will not be likely to succeed, the idea there is that it is more respectful of the toddler's needs and developmental level and also the parents, caregivers, and everyone else at the grocery store and/or post office to not introduce their toddler into a situation that they will likely not do well in. No one enjoys having to navigate and deal with a toddler temper tantrum in the dairy aisle!

There is no one right answer here, only what works best for you and your family. Some toddlers are very easy-going and amenable to days out spent running errand after errand. Other toddlers may be more resistant to days spent getting in and out of the car and going into place after place that requires them to engage in very non-toddler like behavior, such as being quiet and sitting still! Just as with most things parenting, every family is different and must find what works best for them. The most important aspect to keep in mind here, as with many things related to loving discipline, is checking in with ourselves to see if we are guiding our toddlers positively and respectfully.

Building Relationships

Parent-child relationships are very important to toddler development. It is the first model of relationships that most children have, so how we are with our tiny toddlers will set the foundation for how our toddlers will interact in relationships with others throughout their lives.

Secure attachment, or the positive relationship that a child has with their parents/caregivers that they know they can depend on their parents/caregivers for physical and emotional support and safety. The presence of this type of relationship plays a strong role in a child's sense of safety and independence.

As toddlers learn how to build relationships based on their relationships in these early, formative years, there is a piece of the puzzle that is sometimes lost: that of the father figure. Families can be constructed in many different forms, including families that have a mother and a grandmother as the two primary caregivers, families that have a single mother as the primary caregiver, families that have two mothers as the primary caregiver, and many, many more combinations. It is not that there must be the person that shares DNA present in our toddler's life, but there needs to be a person that is able to model what a healthy and successful male relationship looks like (just as it is important to have a person that is able to model what a healthy and successful female relationship looks like). If the biological father is not present, and there is no stepfather, or close uncle or grandfather available to help model this healthy and successful male relationship, then a family can seek out other ways to be sure this relationship is modeled, such as with a close family friend.

The importance here is in recognizing that for young girls, their relationship with a father figure is a model for their future relationships with males and what sort of treatment and relationship they will seek out and tolerate. For young boys, their relationships with a father figure is a model for their future selves, as they often model themselves after this primary male influence. Without a strong father figure, young boys will often model themselves after the nearest available male, which may or may not be the sort of influence that parents and caregivers want their young boys to be influenced by.

Becoming more aware of how we are structuring our toddler's lives, from their environment to the people in it, is an important part of disciplining toddlers in a loving way. Understanding their psychology and how we can better relate to them respectfully goes a long way to ensuring we are creating a loving environment that contributes to parents and caregivers abilities to guide and teach our toddlers well.

Useful Information and Tips for This Chapter

Development phases of the baby

Clinical and developmental psychologists examine this process through the developmental stages through which the child passes in the earliest period:

0-2 months: the child is primarily directed at himself, and in interaction with the environment reacts almost to each person

2-6 months: the child responds directly to family members

6-8 months: strong attachment to the mother, shows clear signs of fear when the mother is not nearby

8-12 months: the child slowly emerges from the symbiotic relationship with the mother, it is important that the mother reacts to the child's independent movements in order not to prevent the separation and individuation of the child that begins at this stage. The child shows separation fears due to emotional separation from the mother and uses "transient objects" (stuffed toys, blankets)

Intellectual development

The intellectual development of a child in the first year takes place through the training of senses and movements. Thus, in the first six weeks, the baby is practicing reflex movements, in order to be able to manage them in the second month. During the third and fourth month, the child repeats actions aimed at exploring one's own body (for example, repeating the same movement by a hand or foot), and from the fourth to the ninth month will repeat acts directed to the external environment (throwing the toy in the same way).

Until the baby turns six months, if the parents pull the toy from her sight, she does not look for it. But at an average age of six months, the baby starts looking for an object that is out of her sight, which means she begins to understand that the objects exist independently of her field of vision.

Incentive of development

From seven to eight months, the child can distinguish the means from the objective and anticipate events, so for example if he cries and mom or dad enters the room, the child ceases to cry because he predicts comforting. When a child begins to crawl, parents can, in a simple way, through the game, encourage him to solve the problem, they can put an obstacle (a larger toy or pillow) between the child and the toy the child is headed to. The child will crawl up to the obstacle, remove it, and reach the desired target. Because of this, the hiding games that children also like at a later age are encouraging the intellectual development of children in a certain way, because they teach that objects exist independently of them and that they can solve the problem and reach the goal.

The emotional and intellectual development of the child is complex and inseparable from the overall physical progress, so all of the mentioned ages are averages, and subject to individual variations. It is only important that parents, in the course of monitoring the development of the child, be directed to induce and encourage their development.

10 Things That Make the Baby Happy

Observing your child and appreciating what makes him happy is one of the ways to strengthen a relationship with a child. These are some of the things that babies love most:

1. Babies like when they are naked

For some babies is enough just to remove their clothes and diaper to calm down. There is a constant connection between the body and the feelings of the baby, and since they can not speak, their body expresses all their feelings. For this reason, babies want to get rid of all tensions and be as free as they can in their bodies. When they are naked, babies seem to receive and express their emotions more easily. They differently see the world around themselves when they are without clothes and it is easier for them to explore and get to know their environment.

2. The babies like to be cuddled

It reminds them of the time spent in the womb, in the stomach of their mother, when they were surrounded by "walls" that protected them and provided shelter. In the first few weeks of life, many babies feel satisfied when their mothers wrap them into the blanket and carry them; they like the sense of intimacy. Gradually, babies feel freer and start making the first safer and more confident movements.

3. Touching your mother's skin

Mother's embrace is the best solution for almost all problems. Many studies have shown that direct contact with the body, more precisely with the skin, between mother and baby, balances the baby's body temperature and heart rate, and helps the secretion of endorphins and oxytocin hormones, the hormone of love, not only in the baby but also in the mother. In contact with the mother's skin, the nerve system of the newborn relaxes and thus improves the relationship between mother and child, since both feel close and loved.

4. Monotone sounds

Monotone sounds (sound of the motor, washing machine ...) resembles the sounds that baby has been listening for 9 months in the mother's stomach, and it relaxes them. These sounds that reach the baby are mostly muted, as well as the sounds in the stomach.

5. Music

Music is a stimulus for learning: its high and low tones stimulate neural connections, reorganize the brain and, depending on the type of music (classical, modern ...), help the baby in different ways. Harmonic sounds dominated by high tones are preparing a baby for learning. Low tone melodies relax the baby. The baby feels the voices of her parents as music: higher tones are mommy's and lower daddy's.

6. Mom's scent

Many babies who have trouble sleeping relax when mom put a piece of her clothes into the crib. The first thing newborn feels with his senses is parents smell. The sense of smell is associated with the urge to survive, and for newborns, it is crucial to recognize and remember the smell of their parents after birth; without it, it is helpless. Although they do not see well, newborns can recognize their parents by smell. The mother's arms are one of the happiest places for the baby - she feels the smell of her mother and knows she is safe.

7. Walks

Many kids require more attention and are crying more when they are at home than when they are outdoors. Babies feel that air is not the same inside and outside the house; they notice the difference between the air in motion and stagnant air from indoors. Apart from the air, the sounds and smells differ from the outside. Senses of hearing and smell are very developed since birth, for this reason a walk around the park is the best way for a baby to relax by feeling new smells and listening to new sounds - all this develops an adventurous spirit in the baby!

8. Babies like to stick everything in their mouths

The mouth is the baby's "third eye": they help the baby to meet the world that surrounds her. When a baby is sucking various objects, she reveals their taste, texture, density, weight ... She gets information that she could not get only by observing the object. During the first two years of life, a baby's mouth is a kind of scanner that helps them create an image in their brain of what is out there.

9. Rocking

Rocking consists of uniform, rhythmic movements that connect the baby with their senses with safety and balance. On the one hand, rocking develops deeper neural connections, and on the other hand, monotonous and predictable rhythms are associated with the stability of the child. The baby gets the security and confidence in her mother, and the more familiar her rhythm is, the more relaxed she is, she releases more endorphins and more quickly adapt to the environment.

10. Mommy's voice

Mother's voice is one of the things that contain everything that makes the baby feel peaceful: it contains music, high tones that stimulate learning, and most importantly - the desire to communicate with the baby. Every time a mother turns to the baby, the baby registers a number of emotions, which awake her desire to learn to speak. As soon as they become capable of it, the babies answer you with giggly. Communicating with parents is their greatest wish.

Chapter 2: Toddler Discipline Techniques - Language Strategies For Stressed Parents

More often than not, restraining toddlers includes child rearing worry for guardians. It is difficult managing toddlers who are shouting, kicking, yelling and pitching every one of those temper fits. Guardians must apply toddler discipline techniques to be capable for them to raise polite toddlers and appreciate child rearing life.

One essential viewpoint that guardians can concentrate on is the utilization of compelling correspondence. By utilizing language strategies, guardians can pass on discipline focuses on their toddlers.

Guardians must be informed of utilizing positive words when conversing with their toddlers. Abstain from using mark words, for example, terrible, devious and other negative depictions. Toddlers can be influenced that psychologically like prompting low confidence. Rather than saying "stop" and "no," guardians must state what precisely they need their toddlers to do. The words "Stop" and "no" are inadequate if use as often as possible. Spare these words for essential occasions, not with your everyday conversations with your toddlers. Toddlers, same like grown-ups, would almost certainly tune if we guide them, not what we don't need them to do.

When addressing your toddlers particularly amid their hissy fits, guardians must keep quiet and ought not to raise their voice. Regardless of whether guardians are not utilizing negative words, the way of expressing can include or decrease the viability of your toddler discipline endeavors. By shouting more often than not, you are modifying your toddler's mind that it is ordinary and he will be slanted not to hear you out additional.

Guardians can utilize specific language patterns that can be used as everyday conversations with toddlers relying upon the circumstances. These language patterns as toddler discipline techniques include the use of neuro-phonetic programming or NLP. By joining NLP ideas, guardians can without much of a stretch convince their toddlers to get things done.

Step by step instructions to Handle Toddler Discipline

One thing that most guardians don't care to do is discipline their kid, mainly if they are only a toddler. I despise toddler discipline however you can't maintain a strategic distance from it if your kid is severely carried on generally how they would gain directly from off-base?

When I was a youngster, I used to get a decent hitting now and again however at this point I understand that I merited it, yet in the present society, guardians look to different types of toddler discipline to abstain from giving physical control.

Indeed, even as a toddler in their all-around beginning times of life, you ought to set a couple of essential guidelines. Not very many, around 4 or 5 is a decent figure. One thing you ought to

Keep in mind when setting these principles is that you should be steadfast with them. If you set standards, at that point you should remain by them generally there isn't much point. Disclose to your toddler what the rules are and after that when they break one go over the norm once more, every time they do as such. Your toddler ought to likewise understand that you being the parent they need to do what you state.

Toddlers are polite just as now and again severely acted. When they are polite at that point to give your kid applause, and this will strengthen to them that with excellent conduct they get applauded yet with offensive conduct they will get disciplined.

At the point when your toddler gets out of hand at that point demonstration with a firm definitive voice. If they are approached to kill the TV for instance and they won't, be firm when you state "Do as I state," don't say it with anger. If your toddler discipline isn't working and your toddler is insubordinate don't give in. When you give in this is a sure sign to them that they will act insubordinate next time and get their direction.

One compelling type of toddler discipline is the break. If your toddler is resistant, at that point, you can send them to a break room or a spot. Let your toddler knows that they should remain in the broken place so they can consider their conduct.

Disclose to your toddler they will stay on the break spot or room until they are prepared to come and sit and chat with you about their behavior. This is a necessary type of discipline yet well-known as it is viable.

Effective Toddler Discipline Through Positive Language Communication

First-time guardians will in all likelihood experience serious difficulties managing the conduct of their toddlers. If they are not well-educated regarding the learning of how to discipline their toddlers effectively, it can genuinely be unpleasant. Toddlers can start to display unsafe

practices when they achieve two years of age. They are not called "awful twos" in vain. The practices related to hissy fits can presumably be experienced up to their seventh year. It is incredibly significant for guardians to be outfitted from the get-go with the necessary systems for them to have a head-begin restraining their toddlers.

One significant angle that guardians need to know in toddler discipline is the best possible utilization of language when speaking with their toddlers. The selection of words can have a significant effect. It is essential to utilize positive words more often than not when conversing with your toddlers, particularly when you are making your discipline talk.

Studies have demonstrated that you will have higher achievement in getting your message comprehended by toddlers, yet also with grown-ups if you utilize positive words rather than negative terms. Notice how a basic "Don't do that" isn't always effective in ceasing your toddlers in accomplishing something awful? You may be increasingly active if you instruct me. Much the same as grown-ups, toddlers will almost certainly tune if we guide them, as opposed to disclosing to them what not to do.

Guardians ought to likewise cease from depicting their toddler's as awful, irksome, underhanded and other unfavorable terms. Toddlers can be influenced mentally that can lead them to carry on more contrarily. It can likewise prompt low confidence.

Toddler Discipline - 5 Steps to Better Toddler Behavior

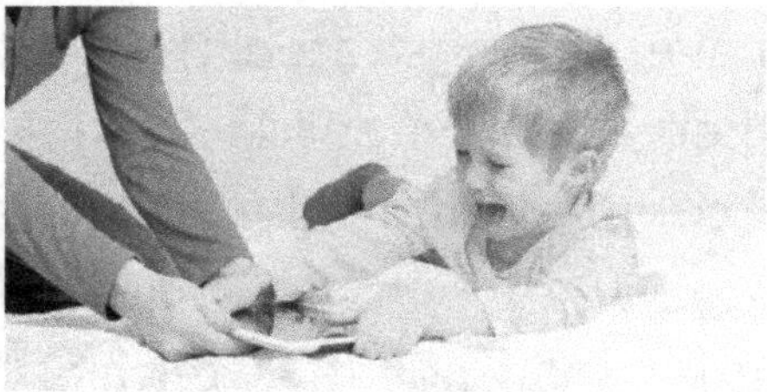

Toddler discipline is a standout amongst essential prerequisites in the advancement of a respectful tyke, yet for some guardians, it very well may be an overwhelming assignment. So here are five parts of the discipline, which have demonstrated to be exceptionally useful in building up a healthy relationship and reinforce the security among toddler and parent.

Break

This is a standout amongst the most popular types of restraining a young tyke. The young "offender" is sent to a corner or the "insidious spot" for a period. It is significant that this time isn't excessively long, permit 1 minute for every time of age. You may need to remain over them; however ideally with your back or side to them, so they can't draw in with you.

When the time has slipped by, remind your toddler, in everyday language, what they did and stress that if they rehash it, they will confront some other break.

It is significant that discipline must occur at the season of the occurrence so you should be set up to discipline them notwithstanding when far from home. Do it because of the sight of other individuals, so the little one's confidence isn't hurt.

Diversion and Diversion

A standout amongst the best approaches to discipline a toddler is by redirection. You rapidly occupy them from what they are planning to do and redirect them to something "more secure" and progressively positive, for example, helping you around the house. Along these lines, they will live it up as opposed to going down the course prompting inescapable "inconvenience."

Disregarding Temper Tantrums

Hissy fits are times to show an extreme feeling. It is significant the toddler rapidly discovers that their fits won't deal with the circumstance or you. There are two different ways that you can accomplish this (a) by overlooking their conduct totally or (b) by telling them that you don't prefer to see their dishonest behavior and recommending that when they have completed, you will converse with them about it.

With training, you will most likely rapidly defuse the circumstance so you can talk about it with them quietly and calmly.

Uplifting feedback

It has appeared encouraging feedback works much preferred with toddlers over discipline. Rather than always saying "no" to them, when they foul up, discover the things that they do well and reward them with loads of positive criticism like much love. Make an effort not to turn into the habitual scolder.

Defining Rules and Limits

Toddlers are generally curious and bold, so they need standards and limits set for them to keep them sheltered and out of inconvenience. They feel increasingly safe and cherished when someone helps them to comprehend why these standards have been set. It is significant that the rules you set are basic and straightforward for the toddler to get it. They should likewise be connected reliably, so the youngster does not end up befuddled.

These five different ways of empowering and creating toddler discipline have worked for some guardians and will ideally work for you. This is only the begin. Toddlers grow up all around rapidly, and there is significantly more than you can figure out how to make the "growing up" years a glad and remunerating background for both parent and kid. Luckily there is a ton of incredible counsel accessible online.

Toddler Discipline - A Big Challenge Awaits

One of life's biggest challenges is to turn into a parent. Child-rearing is an expertise that you learn en route. It's frequently a rough street of high points and low points. A few people will discover child rearing simpler than others; however, to be a good parent not just intends to demonstrate your toddler love; it additionally wants to show them the contrasts among excellent and evil. This is generally done as toddler discipline. If your toddler fouls up, at that point restraining them reveals to them they have fouled up. The equivalent if they do good, we demonstrate to them that what they have done is good by compensating them in some structure.

With any test, particularly child rearing, you will have your good minutes and your terrible minutes. Things might go quickly at a certain point, at that point be turned entirely on its head the following.

One point that guardians can battle with is toddler discipline. This is any parent, not merely unseasoned parents. One type of toddler discipline may take a shot at one toddler; however, it will be completely ineffective on another.

This is the test you face, realizing what types of discipline will work for your toddler and what won't work. It's about experimentation.

All toddlers need discipline. Without discipline how are they to comprehend what is correct and what's up? It additionally instructs them that they are in charge of their activities. It tells them about what is proper behavior and what is poor practice.

One thing you have to recollect when utilizing your picked type of discipline is that anyway; your toddler reacts to it, you should remain quiet. This encourages you to stay in charge and demonstrates that you are the manager, and any fits or temper tantrums your toddler may toss, you are the one that is in charge.

Anyway, much you wind up restraining your toddler, you should, in any case, show them adore and love, regardless of how troubled inside they may make you feel. Your toddler has to realize you love them, and if you have a good bond, at that point, the odds are that the better acted your toddler will be, and that fulfills everybody.

Toddler Discipline

Toddler discipline dependably is by all accounts at it more terrible when you are out with your toddler. The fits of rage, crying and behavior issues become risky and once in a while make them mull over going anyplace. These behavior issues happen in the specialist's office, at an eatery, at the recreation center... anyplace you dare to go. Taking everything into account, by what method may you wipe out or if nothing else re-direct the fits, crying and behavior issues? Toddlers can't avoid being toddlers. They are investigating and learning. They are requesting and obstinate. It may be as necessary as having a couple of things available to you to enable you to keep your toddler involved and engaged. Toddler discipline when in a hurry can be contained by having:

An Activity Bag... This pack ought to provide a different toy, shading book and pastels, a storybook, simple things and exercises the toddler can do.

Portable DVD Player... This portable DVD player will engage a toddler for at any rate of 15-30 minutes.

Toddler DVDs... Intuitive DVDs and motion pictures for youngsters

These proposals do include you conveying and transporting things or sacks wherever you go. In any case, these choices will help with shortening the fits of rage, crying or potentially behavior issues. Depending on these instruments will help make your excursion an agreeable one with your toddler. You will have the chance to cooperate with your toddler, show them the proper behavior out in the open and permit everyone around you to have a charming excursion also.

Presently you can anticipate going anyplace with your toddler and having choices to keep your little one engaged, occupied and glad while in a hurry!

Dealing with Toddlers - Parenting Tips in Dealing with Your Toddlers

Managing toddlers may not be as easy as it appears as fits of rage in toddlers are among the difficulties of most guardians, for what it's worth in this phase your little one might test your understanding. Your toddlers may have their very own standards, they won't tune in or they may all of a sudden have their specific manner of conveying everything that needs to be carried like shouting, along these lines figuring out how to manage them at this stage is significant.

At ages one to three, children become keen on numerous things, and they want to investigate and copy. You may discover them opening drawers, moving into anything, blending the fishbowl, playing with your pets, looking into the substance of your tote and you may even observe your little girl covering her lips with your lipstick if she has seen you do that.

In this phase where kids love to investigate things and pitch a few fits frequently, here are a few hints to help you in managing toddlers and their conduct.

Make your home a protected spot for your little child. You may not thoroughly prevent a baby from investigating things, climbing furniture and finding things around them as these are a piece of her improvement. It won't be great also to leave your little child unsupervised while they do their job. You can manage this securing thing that can hurt him, fix broken furnishings, spread electric attachments, continue clearing items out of his span and keep a watchful gaze over him.

Ignore their fits of rage. In managing toddlers, you need to comprehend that they, for the most part, hear you out when they have fits, so you must have vast amounts of tolerance. You don't need to surrender to his requests dependably. Regularly, toddlers who pitch their fits are just looking for consideration and one approach to manage it is to disregard them until he quiets down and stop.

Distract him, abandon him or do him your alternatives rely upon the circumstance. If he opposes on getting something he needs, you might need to give choices as well. Without a doubt, it very well may be hard notwithstanding for children to get need you required them to have. Offer an elective toy or another choice of vegetable if he doesn't need the first. If you are openly, obviously, you can't abandon him there. You need to complete him if he isn't quieting down.

Classify which are debatable and non-debatable with regards to managing toddlers and their fits of rage. When your little child demands to have that pink dress over the one you are making her wear, at that point don't sweat it. However, with regards to increasingly significant issues that worry his security, his wellbeing, and so forth then you should not give in, and you should adhere to that standard.

Try to decide the distinctive activating elements of his fits of rage. Frequently, they would go into fits of anger if they are drained, hungry or lazy, so you might need to address them first. Likewise, ensure you are giving your child proper nutrition as this also can trigger the emotional episodes of your little child.

Toddlers and their fits of rage can be a trial of your understanding yet as all these are a piece of their advancement and can be inescapable, you can discover routes in making this stage somewhat more straightforward for you and your tot.

Chapter 3: Things To Consider When Disciplining Toddlers

Many parents attest to the reality that disciplining a toddler is like facing constant uphill battles. These little bundles of delight can turn to extremely stubborn kids who test the patience limits of caregivers and adults around them.

It is also the phase of childhood where they begin to assert their independence. One of their first words is “No,” affirming the toddlers’ love to do things in their way. They enjoy running away to escape. Normal toddlers are full of energy. They run, jump, play, explore, and discover everything that interests them. They love to use the sense of touch, exploring things with their senses. Because toddlers are easily stimulated by what they see or hear, their impulsive nature can make them clumsy and touch things. Parents need to teach their children safe ways to touch or handle things and not to touch hot objects.

Although raising a toddler entails a lot of hard work, seeing your child grows and develops his skills is fascinating. However, because of the developmental changes that rapidly happen during the toddler stage, it is necessary to use a disciplinary approach that will foster the child's independence while teaching him socially appropriate behavior and other positive traits.

All too often, there is an assumption that parenting techniques apply to all, and kids will react or respond in a similar pattern. But every child has his own set of traits. They are in his DNA, which he inherited from his parents. Some toddlers are shy or even-tempered, while others are outgoing and have aggressive natures.

By understanding the child's special personality and natural behavior, you can help him adjust to the real world. It is necessary to work with his personality and not against it, taking into account the following factors that you need to consider when disciplining your toddler. Giving proper care and nourishment, providing positive and healthy activities, and instilling positive discipline is vital to his physical, mental, emotional, social, and behavioral growth..

A. Temperament and Behavior

Temperament is defined as the heritable and biologically based core that influences the style of approach and response of a person. The child's early temperament traits usually predict his adult temperament.

The child's **behavior** is the outcome of his temperament and the progress of his emotional, cognitive, and physical development. It is influenced by his beliefs about himself, about you, and the world in general. While it is inborn and inherent, there are certain ways to help your toddler manage it to his advantage.

Nine dimensions or traits related to temperament:

The activity level pertains to the amount of physical motion that your toddler demonstrates, while engaged in some activities. It also includes his inactive periods.

- Is your child a restless spirit who cannot sit still for so long or want to move around?
- Is your toddler the quiet, little one who enjoys playing alone or watching TV?

Rhythmicity refers to the predictability or unpredictability of physical and biological functions which include hunger, bowel movement, and sleeping.

- Does your child thrive on routine and follow regular eating or sleeping patterns?
- Does he display unpredictable behavior and dislike routine?

ATTENTION SPAN AND PERSISTENCE are the skills to remain focused on the activity for a certain period.

- Does your toddler stick to complete a task?
- Is he easily frustrated and look for another activity?

INITIAL RESPONSE (APPROACH OR WITHDRAWAL) refers to the reaction to something new and unfamiliar. It describes his initial feelings to a stimulus like a new person, place, toy, and food. His reaction is shown by his mood or facial expressions like smiling or motor activity, such as reaching for a toy or swallowing food. Negative responses include withdrawal, crying, fussing, pushing away, or spitting the food.

- Is he wary or reluctant around unfamiliar situations or strangers?
- Does he welcome new faces and adjust comfortably with new settings?

THE INTENSITY OF REACTION is associated with the level of response to any event or situation. Toddlers respond differently to events around them. Some shrieks with happiness or giggle joyfully, others throw fits, and many barely react to what is happening.

- Do you always experience trying to guess the reaction of your child over something?
- Does your child explicitly show his emotions?

ADAPTABILITY is the child's ability to adjust himself to change over time.

- Is your child capable of adjusting himself to sudden changes in plans or disruptions of his routine?
- Does he find it difficult to cope up with changes and resist it as much as he can?

DISTRACTIBILITY is the level of the child's willingness to be distracted. It relates to the effects of an outside stimulus on your child's behavior.

- Can your child focus on his activity despite the distraction that surrounds him?
- Is he unable to concentrate when there are people or other activities going on in the environment?

QUALITY OF MOOD is related to how your child sees the world in his own eyes and understanding. Some react with acceptance and pleasure while other children scowl with displeasure just "because" they feel like it.

- Does he display mood changes constantly?
- Does he generally have a happy disposition?

SENSORY THRESHOLD is linked to sensitivity to sensory stimulation. Children who are sensitive to stimulation requires a careful and gradual introduction to new people, experiences, or objects.

- Is your child easily bothered by bright

lights, loud sounds, or food textures?

- Is he totally undisturbed with such things and welcome them as such?

There are three main types of toddlers:

- **Active or Feisty Toddlers-** These children have a tremendous amount of energy, which they show even while inside the uterus of their mothers, like lots of moving and kicking. As an infant, they move around, squirm, and crawl all over the place. As toddlers, they climb, run, jump, and even fidget a lot to release their energy. They become excited while doing things or anxious around strangers or new situations.

They are naturally energetic, joyful, and loves fun. But when they are not happy, they will clearly and loudly say it. These toddlers are also quite obstinate and hard to fit in regular routines.

To help him succeed:

? Acknowledge his unique temperament

and understand his triggers.

- Teach him self-help skills to get going if his energy is low or how to calm down when his activity level is very high. Some simple and effective ways to calm down are counting from 1 to 10, taking deep breaths, doing jumping jacks to get rid of excess energy, and redirecting him to other activities.
- Set a daily routine that includes play and other activities that enhance his gross motor movements. Provide him with opportunities to play and explore safely. It is necessary to childproof your home.
- Insist on nap time. An afternoon nap will refresh his body and mind, preventing mood swings and tantrums.
- Do not let him sit in front of a television or do passive activities. Break the boredom by taking him outside and play in the outdoors.
- Become a calming influence. Understand how your temperament

affects his temperament and find ways to become a role model.

- **Passive or Cautious Toddlers-** These children prefer activities that do not require a lot of physical effort, move slower, and want to sit down more often. They are slow-to-warm-up when meeting new people and often withdraw when faced with an unfamiliar situation. They also need ample time to complete their tasks.

To help him succeed:

- If your child is less active, set guidelines or deadlines that will prompt him to finish the given tasks.
- Invite him to play actively by using interesting noises, bright toys, or gentle persuasion.
- Always accentuate the positive. Be generous with praise and words of encouragement when they display efforts or achieve simple milestones.

- **Flexible or Easy Toddlers** - These children are very adaptable, generally calm, and happy. But sometimes, they are easily distracted and need a lot of reassurance and love from you.

To help him succeed:

- Be realistic and expect mood changes when something is not smooth-sailing. Do not be too hard on the child when he displays unusual outburst.
- Provide him with interactive activities and join him. Sometimes, it is easy to let him play his own devices because of his good-natured personality. It is necessary to introduce other options to enhance his skills.
- Read the signs and find out the reasons for subtle changes in the behavior and attitude toward something. Be observant and have a special time for him.

B. Nine Methods for Toddler Discipline

Instilling discipline is a dilemma for most parents, especially the new ones. They look for the most effective approach to raise well-mannered and positive children who are capable of coping up with the challenges in the real world.

Technically, there is no right or wrong approach except the punitive ways that scar children for life. All it takes is to find the right disciplinary method that will work with your child's inherent personality, behavior, and temperament.

Here are some simple methods that are widely used by parents all over the world:

Commendation & Encouragement

Praise and encouraging words always bring positive outcomes, motivating toddlers to show good behavior. Giving your child small rewards or applause when he does something commendable will encourage him to continue improving his skills. Praising good behaviors will make him repeat the same thing again and again to gain your approval and praise.

Rethinking

Changing the tone of your discourse or reframing your thoughts often results in a positive reaction. Instead of giving an instruction that uses "don't do that" or "get that", rethink your strategy to mirror a solicitation. It is better to use the phrases "would you...if it is fine with you?"

Remember that your toddler is not a mini-you. It also helps to view things from his perspective. For instance, he does not want to sit in the child car seat, you may say- "I know that you do really like sitting in your car seat, but it is essentially like this seat belt that I have. They make us both safe." In this manner, you are teaching him the importance of being safe by using proper tools.

Disregard

Disregarding fits or tantrums intentionally sends a clear signal to your child that you are not affected by his behavior and you will not succumb to his whims. To make it more effective, all other adults in your home must know this strategy to discipline and break the child's tantrum habits. It may seem harsh, but refraining to engage or respond to your child's temper tantrum is one of the keys to curb the habit.

Ignoring or looking the other way is an effective way to curb the child's habit of doing something naughty just to get your attention. Avoid meeting his eyes, glaring, or getting angry because it signifies that your attention to him. You need to act like you are not disturbed by his behavior, making him realize that screaming or throwing tantrums will not make you yield to his desires.

Break

It is also called a time-out, a popular technique most parents used to discipline their children. The idea is to send him to a certain "cozy spot" in your home, a particular place that is safe and free from stimulation or distraction and let him reflect on his behavior. It is important that you can see him and ensure his safety. After a certain time of the break, talk about what happened, giving him time to explain and admit his misdeed.

A good rule of thumb for setting a time limit must correspond to the age of the child, so if your kid is 2 years old, enforce a 2-minute break. However, use this method sparingly and avoid making him feel isolated or alone.

Substitute & Distraction

If your child has this habit of hitting something inside the house like banging his toy on the table, distract him before he can do it. You can attract his attention by showing him something. Young children are easy to distract because they usually have a short attention span. You can also substitute his toys, redirecting him into something more interesting.

Toddlers do not understand why they are being disciplined. Divert his attention with another activity or toy that will interest him. Calling his name aloud grabs his attention, then once his eyes are fixated on you, show him something that will compel him to come to you.

Offer Decisions

Letting your child takes part in simple decision-making like what color of the shirt he wants to wear gives him a sense of pride and control. It boosts his confidence and lessens the occurrences of power struggles. By involving him in the process, you ease the transition and make him proud of making a choice.

These last three methods should be avoided as much as possible.

Surrendering to fits of rage

Your little child will be persistent and throw fits of rage to make you give in to his demands. If you yield the first time, it becomes a ticket for him to attempt another try. It is the toddler's control strategy and can be prevented by not yielding to his unreasonable requests that will compromise his health and safety.

Raising your voice. When is it appropriate?

Some parents admit that one time or another, they yell at their children. Studies show that yelling is one of the discipline techniques that can make behavior issues worse, undermining the parent and child bond. It also loses its effectiveness over time when your child begins to tune you out when you do it regularly.

When is yelling necessary? Expressing your emotions aloud can be positive for you and your child, helping him develop empathy and realize that he has upset you. However, be mindful of your language. Instead of "you" statements, use "I" statements like "I am feeling disappointed because you won't share your toys with your brother" rather than "You are not being nice!"

It is also necessary to be aware of your inner feelings and behavior. Sometimes, you bellow out because you are in a bad mood or tired, and not because your child has done something awfully wrong.

Punishment

Punishment in all forms, including spanking, caning, and beating is a big NO. It has been a thing in the past, used by parents to control their children, but many studies showed that it caused long-term disdain and misery. Spanking, for example, even occasional, can lead to the development of childhood anxiety and makes your child think that it is fine to hit.

Children learn to be afraid of the consequences when caught, but do it anyway when you are not present. If you say, "Don't make me catch you doing it again or you will be grounded!", he may interpret the act as not inappropriate and he just needs to be careful so you will catch him doing it. The result does not resolve the behavior problem and becomes ineffective in helping the child make better choices or learn self-control. There is also a consistent result in various surveys that punishment pushes children to spend more time in avoidance behavior and being rebellious.

Chapter 4: The Common Mistakes That Parents Make And How To Fix Them

Disciplining your toddlers alone is not alone. You must also avoid the common pitfalls of parenting. Many of these blunders do not just decrease the effectiveness of the discipline that you impose on your toddler but may even encourage your toddlers to misbehave. Here are the common mistakes that many parents make when disciplining their children.

Being Aggressive

Some parents simply give up and become aggressive. The problem with being aggressive is that the children learn nothing except fear. They do not get to understand the value that you want them to learn. Instead, they obey you out of fear. Studies also show that toddlers who have experienced aggressive or abusive parents are likely to grow aggressive as well. Being aggressive does not just mean spanking your kids, but it also includes using highly offensive words and threatening words. It is important to note that you are dealing with a toddler and being aggressive is the worst thing you can do.

Comparing Yourself with Other Parents

Stop comparing yourself with other parents. How they discipline their kids is their problem. If one of your friends tells you that slapping your kid in the face is effective, even if he could prove it, do not follow the advice right away. After all, according to various studies, slapping or hitting your kids is not an effective way to discipline them.

Comparing your Child with Other Children

It is wrong to compare your child with other children, except if it will be something that will make him feel good about himself. Would you like your child to compare you in terms of money with a parent who is much richer than you are? Of course not. In the same way, you should not compare your child with other children. Your toddler is unique in his way, and you should appreciate him as he is.

Lying

Some parents lie to their toddlers to make them obey. Although this may work from time to time, it also has bad consequences. In a case study of a mom from New Jersey with a 2-year-old daughter, it so happened that one day when her child did not want to get in the car, she pointed at her neighbor's house nearby and told her kid that it was a daycare center full of troglodytes from a scary TV show. She told her daughter that she had two choices, to get in the car or be left alone in the house with a threat of being attacked by creepy cavemen. Of course, her daughter finally gave in and entered the car. Now, if you look at what happened, it will seem that it was successful. There was no shouting or spanking or anything that took place. However, the problem here occurred after the incident. Following the case study, the mom's daughter began to have a fear of daycare centers, thinking that such places have scary cavemen. As you can see, although the mother was able to make her child get into the car, the consequence was worse. Therefore, instead of lying, the best way is, to be honest, and be emphatic.

Yelling

You do not have to yell at your toddler just to get your point across. According to Dr. Alan Greene, a pediatrician and member of the clinical faculty at Stanford University School of Medicine, if you lose control and start yelling, your kid will also do the same. Now, this does not mean that your kid is intentionally disrespecting you. This only proves that your child is having a hard time with you because you cannot understand each other. Therefore, you must keep your voice quiet yet firm. Eyes contact also helps.

Thinking that You Understand Your Toddler

The truth is that you cannot always understand your toddler. This is simply because toddlers do not think the same way as adults do. You simply cannot tell exactly how certain things have an impact on your toddler's feelings and thoughts. More importantly, you do not know just up to what degree. Therefore, do not be too hard on your toddler.

Raising the Child, you Want

Do not impose your life or your will upon your toddler. Your child has his own life. Let him pursue whatever he wants. Let him paint his dreams and believe in them. Focus on the child whom you already have and not the idea of a child in your mind whom you would wish to have. Your child may not be wired the way you would want him to be, and this is normal. Let your child have his chance in life. Let him believe and live his dreams.

Correcting Everything at the Same Time

Many parents try to correct all the inappropriate behaviors of their child, and they expect a toddler to be able to do it within a short period. This is a very unreasonable expectation. Even you cannot change your bad manners and behaviors quickly, so do not expect your toddler to be able to do it much more than you can. Not to mention, most parents' complaints about their toddlers are normal behaviors (or misbehaviors) for a toddler.

You must learn to pick your battles, and do not even attempt to win everything at the same time. You may start with the behavior that you consider to be the most serious and requires attention. Once you have corrected it, then you can move to another. Of course, you should discipline your child with every opportunity that presents itself. But, learn to focus on a particular behavior, so you can also gauge the effectiveness of the technique or techniques that you are using.

Long Explanations

Long explanations do not work on toddlers. You will only seem like talking gibberish after a few minutes. Do not forget that toddlers have a short attention span; therefore, long explanations do not work well with them. For example, you do not have to lecture your toddler why eating cookies before bedtime is not good for her teeth. She will learn that when the right time comes. Instead, just say, "No cookies." You do not have to explain so much. After all, toddlers are not meant to be very logical. They do not care so much about explanations. Of course, this rule is subject to exceptions, such as when the toddler himself wants to know the reason behind something or when giving an explanation appears to be the best course of action.

Bribe

Do not bribe your toddler just to make him do what you want. Otherwise, he will always ask for it, which could be a problem in the long run. In a case study of a mom in Montclair, New Jersey, she offered her daughter a piece of chocolate if she (her toddler) would eat her meal. It worked well. Her daughter finished her meal quickly. Up to this point, it would seem that bribing is also effective. However, what happened here was that after that dinner, the daughter would always ask her mother to give her a piece of chocolate so that she would finish her meal.

Instead of bribing your child, the suggested way is to help her realize the importance of food. Using the case as mentioned earlier study, the better way would be to tell her child that she will get hungry late in the evening if she eats so little and that she will not be healthy, which could make her sick. If you face a similar problem with your child, you can tell her about the health benefits of the food, like it could make her skin more beautiful, make her taller or smarter, and others — but do not lie.

Not Asking Questions

Toddlers usually have so many questions. As a parent, you tend to answer your question as much as you can. It is worth noting that you should not lie to your child when he asks questions. However, you can make silly answers, but be sure that he knows that it is a joke when you do so. Also, avoid giving creepy answers or those that will tend to scare your child. So, avoid answers that relate to ghosts and other scary stuff. However, parents get too caught up with answering their child's countless questions that they miss another important thing to do: to ask their child questions.

If you can take the time to ask your toddler questions, even crazy and illogical ones, you might just be surprised by the answers that you might hear. Toddlers have a powerful imagination and are very curious and open to almost everything. By asking questions to your child, you will also get to understand how he thinks, and even appreciate how young he truly is — so all the more reason why you should never be aggressive or harsh on your toddler.

Chapter 5: Learning To Communicate With Toddlers

What a daunting task, the awesome responsibility of raising toddlers. Communication is one of the key elements to every successful relationship. You must know how to communicate what you are thinking or feeling.

The Power of Speech

Most parents can't wait for that first, precious, no-doubt-about-it word to spring from their baby's lips. It's hard to believe that by the time your child is a preschooler, you'll have a chatterbox who rarely stops talking (even though you sometimes wish he would).

The ability to talk is one of the biggest distinctions between a baby and a young child. Once, all you could do was guess at the reason behind a cry or a whine. But a talker can make his wishes clearer: “Me cold!” “I want a cracker, not a banana!” and possibly even “Change me!” Being able to communicate adds to the heady, swaggering independence that marks these years. The power of speech also lets a young child make sense of the world around him. He can ask “What’s that?” or “Why?” And your answers will teach him more than he previously learned from just the use of his senses.

There are two parts to language development: understanding what is said and speaking. For a while, toddlers understand far more than they can say. In fact, studies have shown that 1-year-olds who aren’t talking much can comprehend just as much as 1-year-olds with extensive vocabularies.

How Speech Evolves

At first, “ba ba” sounds the same as it has for months. Then you’ll notice your child specifically using those sounds to indicate her bottle or a ball. The first clear word may spring forth as early as 7 months or not until 18 months. It's often Mama or Dado., which are, not coincidentally, some of the same syllable combinations that she's been uttering since 7 to 10 months. First words typically are nouns that refer to an important object (Mama, book, bird) or descriptive words (up, more). The first word may also be social (hi, bye-bye). But listen closely. Sometimes the first word is woven into babbling: "Da da ba kitty." Most children begin to talk between 10 and 18 months.

From then on, your child's language skills explode, in both spoken words and comprehension. But the pace at which these skills develop is completely individual. For example, one major study found that the typical range for a 12-month-old's vocabulary is zero to forty words. By the time a child is 24 months old, she may still use only a few words, or more than six hundred. Sometimes a child acquires a new word every day. Just as often, she gets stuck on a vocabulary of only five or six words for months, followed by a burst of new words all at once. This spark, known as the naming explosion, can be fun. Often a child will point at object after object, or ask, “What’s that?”

Early words are often simplified. Ba can mean “bottle,” “Barney,” “let’s play ball,” or all three of those things, at different times of the day. That’s because toddlers tend to leave off the end consonants. Pronunciation can be tricky for them, too. You may also hear your toddler using a single word to stand for many different but related thoughts. For example, “juice” uttered in a cranky way near naptime may be her way of letting you know she’s tired, if she typically has a cup of juice before her nap. Phrased as a question, “juice” may be her way of asking for more. If she spills the juice, she may say “juice” in a negative tone. Show that you understand by picking up on these utterances and expand on them for her: "Uh-oh, the juice spilled. We have to clean that up, don't we?" These are all signs of progress—she's learning about intonation, if not sentence structure.

Around 18 months a child puts two words together to help her express a thought. "Mama book" may mean "That's Mama's book" or "Will you read the book to me?" She'll also begin to describe objects rather than simply label them: "big cow," "wet pants," "blue shirt." Sentences follow between 24 and 30 months: "Look at the big cow," "My pants got wet." By the third birthday, the use of speech grows increasingly sophisticated. A 3-year-old uses tenses (sleep, slept), plurals (blocks, children), and function words (should, who, would, some).

How You Can Help

A child builds his vocabulary on his own, but there are many ways you can encourage that process.

☐ Talk to your child—often. Converse in the car. While you're pushing the stroller, talk about what you see. Talk about the food during meals. Name his body parts while he's getting dressed or having his diaper changed. In general, the more adult language a child hears, the better. Best of all is conversation directed at your child.

☐ Describe what's happening. Narrate what's happening while you cook or go about everyday activities. "Now I'm chopping a carrot. Then I'll put it in the pot. Look at the steam!" This helps a child put words in their appropriate contexts.

☐ Talk slowly. You don't have to exaggerate every word you utter, but do take pains to be clear and succinct. Stick to short sentences and fairly simple language.

☐ Label objects. At first a toddler may not understand when you point to his coat and say coat, but as he hears the word more frequently, he'll get the idea.

☐ Repeat and recast. If she says, “Go house,” repeat it using proper grammar: “Let’s go in the house.” Echoing, “That’s right. It’s cold,” signals to your child that he’s been understood.

☐ Expand on your child's conversation. If she says, “Bird,” you can say, “Yes, look at the pretty red bird. The bird is sitting on a tree.”

☐ Make eye contact. The more a child can see your face, the better he can learn how different sounds are made.

☐ Use proper pronouns. A common parent trap is to refer to yourself in the third person all the time: “Let Mommy help you.” “Daddy can fix it.” But by using I and you properly, you’ll help your toddler learn these important words.

☐ Play word games. Help a young toddler link words and deeds. Say “I’m going to tickle you!” or “I’m going to pull your piggies!” and then do so. To help teach the names of objects, point to various parts of your body (or pictures in a book, or objects in a room) and say what they are. Eventually your child will be able to use the word when you prompt, “What’s that?” And toddlers think silly mix-ups—calling a nose an eye, for example—are a riot. Games that involve talking—such as having pretend conversations on toy telephones—are another great way to make language fun.

The Magic of Reading

Reading to a child is one of the most cozy, enjoyable things you can do together, and the benefits you reap are far greater than the effort required. A child who is read to often gets a head start on talking, thanks to this added exposure to words. He’s learning to make connections

between words, sounds, and meaning, as well as absorbing the cadences and emotional expression of language. You’re also embedding a lifelong love of books and the stories, adventures, and answers within them.

When to begin? Experts say it's never too soon to read to a child. Certainly by a child's first birthday, you should be having regular reading sessions. Bedtime is ideal, because storytelling is calming and can become part of your going-to-sleep ritual. But books should also be available to a toddler throughout the day, right there with his toys. At first you may barely get through a single volume. Your child will want to turn the pages—fast. Or she may want to chew on the book, or fly through one after another. Don't be discouraged by this—it's good. The whole idea is to make books familiar, fun, beloved objects. Actually following a simple story line will come eventually.

Some ways to make reading pleasurable for both of you: Choose books with toddler allure. Best are those that have bright, uncomplicated artwork that varies a lot from page to page, and brief, captivating stories. Repetition and rhymes are favorites. For a 1-year-old, so are books that simply label pictures of objects. Board books encourage a young child to thumb through them easily on his own (or taste them). But variety adds interest: Also make available plastic or cloth books, pop-ups, oversized volumes, and those with textures. (Go easy on the electronic "talking" books, however. Not only are they annoying to listen to, but the noises they make distract a child from fully absorbing the richness of language.) Pick subjects your child shows a special interest in, be it dinosaurs or construction equipment or teddy bears. Older toddlers will begin to enjoy tales on everyday themes they experience, such as going to the doctor or using the potty.

☐ Snuggle. The best place for a toddler to hear a story is right in your lap.

☐ Tell stories apart from books. Repeat nursery rhymes, tell simple Mother Goose stories (like the Three Litde Pigs), sing songs, or make up your own funny sagas featuring your child as a character. Some children like to listen to books on tape during quiet time or in the car.

☐ Attend story hours in public places. Many libraries and bookstores hold them for free. A younger toddler won't sit still, but a 2V6-or 3-year-old may. Before going to a reading where life-size book characters, such as Clifford the Big Red Dog or Barney, make special guest appearances, prepare your child first—their very size may thrill or terrify a tot.

☐ Let your child see you read. Toddlers love to imitate.

☐ Never withhold reading time as punishment. Not even at bedtime when you're at wits' end. Books should have nothing to do with discipline—ever.

Late Talkers

For every 20-month-old chatterbox, there is another child the same age whose speech is limited to just a few words. If your child seems to talk less than his peers, should you worry? Although late talkers tend to make their parents anxious, patience is important. Many children simply talk later than others, and this trait has no bearing on their health or intelligence. Avoid pressuring such a child or quizzing him incessandy, which can backfire and cause feelings of inadequacy.

Verbal milestones

☐ 7-12 months: May say first recognizable words. Begins to mimic the cadence and tone of adult speech.

☐ 12-18: Uses a word to stand for a thought or sentence: "juice" means "I want juice," "bye-bye" means "I'm ready to go."

☐ months Understands many more words and phrases than says.

☐ 18-24 months: By 18 months, can say about fifty words. By 24 months, may know as many as two thousand. Puts two words together: "big dog." Begins to use verbs. Starts to use pronouns, not always correctly: “me hungry.” Adds several new words to working vocabulary each day.

☐ 24-30 months: Regularly uses sentences that are several words long: “No go sleep,” “Want cracker now.” Understands correct use of me and you.

☐ 30-36 months: Vocabulary continues to grow. Uses word order and phrase structures similar to adult speech. Describes in accurate, vivid detail. By 3 years, uses / correctly and can carry on a conversation.

Before 24 months, it’s hard to pinpoint whether there’s even a problem. In fact, experts can’t agree on the point at which delayed speech should warrant worries. By age 2, you’ll certainly want to see definite efforts to communicate through gestures, sounds, or facial expressions, at least. A child who’s not doing some of these things by 1 or who doesn’t have a vocabulary of at least twelve words by IV2 should be examined to rule out physical or developmental problems.

What if no one can understand my child except me?

It's not unusual for the person who spends the most time around a child to best understand the idiosyncrasies of his or her speech. It can be frustrating for the child when Grandma or Daddy doesn't know what he wants. Help others understand by echoing what the child has said. And be patient. Lisps tend to disappear and enunciation will gradually improve.

Several factors may be responsible for a slow-to-talk toddler: Hearing problems. If your child doesn’t look in the direction of sounds or hasn’t uttered a single word by 14 months, tell your pediatrician. A hearing evaluation can identify any problems that may be interfering with normal speech. Persistent ear infections, even if they have ended and the child’s hearing is now normal, may delay speech. Sometimes speech therapy is recommended to help such a child catch up.

☐ Heredity. Research has shown that some children inherit a tendency to late speech development and a generally laconic manner. So if you're naturally tight-lipped, your children may be, too.

☐ Birth order. Later-borns are sometimes slower talkers, especially when they are close in age to older siblings. This may be because firstborns tend to get more undivided attention—and hear more adult conversation. There's also more time to carefully model conversation for beginning talkers. Older siblings often do the talking for the younger ones, too.

Being a multiple. Twins, for example, sometimes develop their own communication system of made-up words, gestures, and facial expressions. Children who are multiples may also receive less individualized attention.

☐ Gender. Boys and girls learn to talk at about the same pace, overall. But at the extreme ends of the spectrum, it's true that the earliest talkers tend to be girls and very late talkers tend to be boys. Researchers are not sure why this is so.

☐ Activity level. It's not uncommon for a child to abandon his talking efforts amidst newfound zeal for walking and running. This usually changes once he masters the physical skills.

☐ A bilingual household. Generally, a child who grows up hearing two languages initially says fewer words in either language than a child exposed to only one. Eventually the bilingual child catches up, however, and can become fluent in both languages by the preschool years.

☐ Prematurity. A preemie's language skills may lag through the third year. By the school years, however, most children who were premature speak as well as their full-term peers.

☐ A developmental disorder. Some children understand language but have trouble getting their mouths to form the proper sounds for coherent speech. This can be corrected with therapy. Others have language disorders that make it difficult for them to understand words. If your toddler isn't talking by 30 months—or if you're worried before then— insist on a professional evaluation by a physician or a speech-language specialist.

Stuttering

All toddlers stammer a bit. It's a by-product of learning to communicate. Your child's excited thoughts may be flying faster than she can lasso them into words. She may be unconsciously stalling for time while searching for a way to describe something. Tiresome though these endless jerky repetitions can be to hear, have patience. Interrupting to rush the speaker along won't help her find the right words any faster. If she really gets stuck, gently invite her to take a deep breath and start over.

Stammers disappear as children grow more fluent and confident as speakers. It's very rare that a permanent stutter will develop, and toddlerhood is too soon to diagnose such a problem.

Chapter 6: Toddler Discipline Tools

When it comes to disciplining your toddler, don't expect things to be easy after the first spanking. There are times when you will need to enforce your discipline on the little one, so here are some tools to help you with the discipline of your toddler:

Help Little Hands –If your little guy or gal is always reaching for things that they know they shouldn't why not direct their hands to things they should grab. Teach them which things they can handle, which they can't, and which to handle with care.

Understanding Junior – You have to use your mind to try to get into his, and you have to try to understand your little one and what he or she is seeing. They are viewing the world for the very first time, so there is no doubt that everything looks new. They may have no idea something is wrong or bad, so it's up to you to let them know.

Diversion Tactics – If there is one thing that can get little Jimmy to stop pulling hair or little Janet to stay out of the kitchen, it is a diversion. It could be a baking project in the dining room, a movie in the TV room, or a spin out in the yard. By diverting them from their intentions, you can control their actions.

Limits – Limits are very important when it comes to toddlers. They are experiencing the world for the first time, so they have no idea what is right and what is wrong. Make sure that the limits you set are easily understood, clearly explained, and always reinforced.

Structures and Schedules – A structure or schedule to your child's day will actually help him or her to stay out of mischief. If they know that something is coming up, they will be thinking about that activity rather than them being bored.

Redirection – Redirect your child's energy into productive things. If they are throwing the ball at their brother, why not have them throw the ball at the net? By giving them a productive output for their energy, you are making it easier for them to be good.

Parent Power – In the end, you are the one that makes the final call, but save that veto power for when you need it. Don't automatically be the authority, but wait until it an important call to put your foot down and say "because Mommy or Daddy said so!"

Chapter 7: Rules And Rewards

On my fridge, I have a board that my kids helped make. On the board are three sections (the number of kids in the house) and in these sections stickers or magnets get stuck. It's high enough for them not to reach and cheat but still low enough for them to see.

These stickers go toward a specific reward. For example, we have dessert every night. Before you have a heart attack, it's only a cookie. Most of the time healthy, homemade ones. Five stickers mean that they get dessert that night. With every chore that is done and with every good deed, they get a sticker.

Establishing Rules for Your Toddler

For toddlers it's a little different because they can't grasp the concept until they are a little older, but we still work with a reward system even with the toddler. We have set rules like putting away toys before leaving a room or eating the food you don't like first. It's not easy to bring these rules into the house without a reward system in place.

Here is a list of rules and rewards we have set up for our own toddler that work:

- Use your inside voice when you are inside the house

Don't you just hate it when you are having a nice afternoon with some friends and suddenly, the kids start yelling and laughing so loud that you can't hear each other when you speak? That is exactly what inside voices are for. As soon as a toddler starts screaming, I put them outside and sit with them. Whenever they want to go inside, I say, "not until you've learned to use your inside voice." It's an effective way to make any toddler, (and child) use their inside voices. Inside is where all the toys are, anyway.

- Do not climb on the furniture

Once they can walk and talk, it's hard to get them to shut up and sit still. The talking I can still handle but the constant climbing? I am a nervous wreck. Not only because it is no place for a toddler to sit on a coffee table, but it's also very dangerous. Tables have sharp corners, chairs are high, and television cabinets contain things more expensive than the toddler's entire room. You don't want them to knock your television off the stand and you sure don't want them to knock the crystal vase from the coffee table. This is an essential rule that must be met with strict consequences.

- Don't open drawers

When I was little, my mother's cousin used to visit with their little child. She was terrible and got away with murder. While my mother and her cousin used to talk, the kid would sneak around and go through everything my mother owned. Sometimes she returned to the conversation with things kids should never see. It got so bad that my mother told her cousin that she shouldn't visit anymore if she brought her child.

It was wrong to despise the child so much because her mother should have taught her better and whenever my mother mentioned something she'd reply with "children will be children." No, ma'am. Children will most definitely not go through a stranger's personal possessions just because their parents are too lazy to teach them any better. This is why this is such an important rule in my house.

- Don't touch anything that doesn't belong to you

Toddlers break things. It's just the way it is. When there's a toddler in the house, it's best just to put away all the nice things and wait until they are older to take them out again. But when you visit someone else, you don't want your child's sticky hands on everything, not to mention the apologies you need to make when your child breaks something. Don't touch anything that isn't yours unless you have permission.

- Don't leave a room without putting your toys away

Toddlers are messy and this carries on through their entire childhood. You have to teach them from a very young age that they need to put everything away before they leave a room to keep everything neat and tidy.

We never had this rule in the house as I was growing up and I feel for my poor mother. With my brother and me so similar in age, we had a ball with every single toy we owned, and I remember the mess that we made like it was yesterday. I vowed that I would never allow my own children to cause me that much of a hassle. It's not hard for them to put the toy away that they were playing with. It will teach them responsibility and give you fewer grey hairs to boot.

- No fighting

In a house with three children and one toddler, it can sometimes get a little heated. No person is the same and when there is even the smallest of disagreements, the entire house explodes into chaos. This kid hits this one with a ball of socks, the other one slams his door shut, the toddler bites and screams at whoever gets in their way. It's like a movie but without the humor.

As parents, we get exasperated. This is when each of them must go downstairs and sit at the bickering table so they can fight to their heart's content. They also get no dessert for a few days. Why? Because they know that there are better ways to settle their differences than to fight. With the tot, it can be a little rough because they can't speak their minds properly yet, so we just put her in a time out after listening to her side of the story (which is usually just a load of babble and incoherent accusations), but it's important to let the toddler know that she is being listened to as well.

Rewarding Good Behavior

It's hard to come up with suitable rewards for your toddler. Some people go overboard with sweets and toys because they can't think about other rewards, they can give their kids. Here is an effective list of rewards that I have tried, tested, and improved to fit my tots and my pocket.

Here are some rewards I like to give my kids:

- Movie of their choice

Who doesn't love a good movie on repeat? The answer is only a tot, but that's okay because at least they ate all their peas instead of tossing them at their brothers. You don't have to sit with the tot the entire time either, they get caught up in the movie and don't notice when you slip away to finish some chores in the kitchen. In general, when a tot wants to watch a movie that they have seen a hundred times, you will tell them no, but if you give it to them as a reward, you can't refuse to let them watch it.

- A trip to the zoo/museum/park

Consider your budget when you are giving out this reward. I encourage children to be outside and to explore so a park is always a good idea. They might even make some new friends while they are there! A zoo and a museum allow your tots to learn new things and words while feeling like they are getting a reward.

- An extra story before bed

Bedtime stories are sometimes too short, and your tot will be asking for "just one more" on more than one occasion. Toddlers love stories and when you do not usually cave and tell them another story, this is a good way to reward them.

- A game

Whether it's a toddler's board game, a puzzle, or a video game, this will be a great reward for any tot. My partner and I are both big gamers and the tot wants to play along whenever we get our headsets out. Needless to say, whatever we are playing is not suitable for a toddler.

Here is where a game on the tablet comes in. They will feel like they are joining in on the fun while not influencing your high score in the slightest. It's both a reward and a way to keep them busy while you are getting some me-time.

- A cookie

The simplest thing to do is to give your child a cookie as a reward but as much as they love that, their weight and health do not. Be careful what sort of treats you give your tot and make sure that they are healthy and good for them. I usually add fruit into the cookies because my tot absolutely detests the texture of the fruit.

Chapter 8: Inspirational Activities To Do With The Child

Practice what you preach

"Mentor and train alongside your children." It is rather inspiring for children to paintings with their parents, instead of taking directions from them." This manner, they will see which you're invested in their success and will view you as an ally. And howdy, perhaps you may research something new, too! So subsequent time they need your assistance with a task, instead of telling them how to do it, leap in and Try to figure out it collectively.

Inspire fingers-on activities

The significance of "stepping into there and operating with your fingers," explaining that there is something almost primal approximately our desire to build and create. Placed away the computer systems and smart phones get a few tools—even only a hammer, nails and timber—and build something together. "You would possibly mild a hearth interior your youngster which you did not recognize existed." you may additionally assist your child connect with and recognize the way of life that previous generations skilled, earlier than video games and the net.

Anticipate more from your children

It can be tempting to over-help if you want to assist your toddler to prevail; however, hand-keeping can backfire and ship the message that she can't do it on her personal. Instead. "Deliver your children duty, and count on more from them. It's terrific what children are capable of do if you push them to take a management function, formulate their thoughts and execute them. Provide them the gear they need and let them run." photo:

Provide the uncooked substances

Lynn Louise Wonders, LPC, RPT-S, RYT, psychotherapist, and director of services at Marietta Counseling for children & Adults MCCA in Marietta, Georgia, notes the significance of stocking your infant's surroundings with substances conducive to creativity. "Preserve such things as clay, confetti, goodly eyes and popsicle sticks reachable and simply available," she advises. Libby Chalk, LMFT, a therapist on the body of workers at MCCA, provides, "in place of turning on the television for younger children, purchase toys that encourage imaginative play, like a dollhouse, train desk, and farm set. No longer handiest does this encourage creativity and abstract questioning, but it additionally affords possibilities to take on new roles and test with teamwork and relationships.

Help them "peer up."

Whilst parental involvement is paramount, it is also vital that children have opportunities to learn with others on their level. "Locate projects and retailers wherein your children can examine collectively with other children," "Peer-to-peer gaining knowledge of is an extremely motivational, exciting manner to learn, and one which reinforces information like no take a look at or reading ever should." searching for extracurricular sports and camps wherein children paintings together in teams to create something, like a science task or music video, or have your kids and their friends brainstorm creative initiatives they can do at home.

Applaud efforts over consequences

Whilst it's tempting to pile on the reward for an activity nicely executed, it's greater critical to encourage children during the process with a purpose to apprehend and interact their intrinsic creativity and ability. "When an infant realizes for himself that he has the potential, capability and recognize-the way to determine it out, his motivation will become a much deeper pool to attract from than whilst he is predicated on external resources to boost him," says Wonders.

Increase your child's comfort region

Learning about distinctive cultures and methods of existence can increase your toddler's thoughts using commencing his eyes to exchange Tools to do things. "Take your children to unfamiliar locations to examine an extraordinary way of life, even if it is to some other side of your very own city," Wonders shows. Or frequently pattern different cultures' cuisines with your kids, and "perform little studies collectively on that subculture. Help your kids see their own international from a distinct factor of view.

Understand that one length does no longer match-all

"Exceptional brains system data in one of kind approaches," explains Wonders, so don't insist that your child create or examine positively if there are other feasible alternatives that may fit better for her. "Brush up on special getting to know styles and help your infant to understand the manner her brain tactics records most correctly." Take this quiz to discover your child's mastering fashion then "be part of innovative forces to find new methods to examine for a test or complete a challenge." you may be acknowledging and validating your baby's strong point even as empowering her to figure out the things that paintings best for her. Photo:

Help them see the big picture

Kids consider the kind of man or woman they need to be in five years, and even write a letter to their destiny self, deliberating such questions as "What do they need to be recognized for? What do they need their buddies to like them for? What type of activities do they want to be involved in or teams do they want to be on? What's going to they spend their time doing during the week and on weekends? Will they have a job? This may be a brilliant platform to begin speak me approximately a way to attain the goals they are putting and what steps they can be taking today," .

Inspire kids to set their bar

Famous tradition and cliques at many colleges generally tend to sell a very slender definition of what is considered "cool," however your kids don't have to shop for into it. "Tell your kids that cool are what they make it, regardless of their pastimes—whether it is soccer, the cello, theater, dance, writing or chess. Tell them that if they work tough, are enthusiastic about what they're doing, and commit absolutely to it, then that activity is cool.

Activities For Children To Help Them Learn Through Play

The right to play is deemed so fundamental to kids' wellbeing that it's far enshrined by way of the UN as a conventional kids' proper. Play is one of the maximum important approaches in which kid's research. It underpins formal gaining knowledge of later in youth; however, it additionally enables the person toddler to expand their self-worth. It strengthens powers of attention, important for a successful destiny inside the schoolroom, and underpins everything from gaining knowledge of social interactions and norms to the beginnings of medical wondering. Play is specifically important for younger infants.. It's significantly the inspiration of early life improvement in terms of language, emotional intelligence and regulation, creativity, and intellectual reasoning.

What Is Play?

Earlier than we consider which sports are nice for assisting kids to research through play, allows deal with: what's play? The e-book 'Einstein by no means used flash playing cards' by using Golinkoff, Hirsh-Pasek, and Eyer, breaks play down into hearth core factors. Play ought to:

Be fun and enjoyable

haven't any set dreams

Be spontaneous and voluntary

contain lively engagement

involve a detail of make-consider

However, some activities have greater playability than others and are really worth establishing their own proper. The adult offers the gap, assets, and time. We name those 'invites to play' – and these are our top 15.

Water Play

Similar to sand play, water play enables kids to test in a secure environment with simple ideas along with quantity. Moreover, water play is exceptional for studying the results of actions. Upload in a few hand-eye coordination and physical strength and water play is a firm favorite.

Dress-Up And Role Play

Let the children loose with a group of dressing-up clothes and props consisting of toy doctor's kits, and permit their imaginations to run wild. Soon you'll find out the budding medical doctor, vet, nurse, astronaut, chef or thespian. Dressing-up allows children to begin to make experience of the person world, roles, and pastimes, in addition to boosting social interaction. Now not least, dressing-up facilitates to enhance the self-care aspects of self-dressing that's essential for primary college existence.

Doll And Character Play

And we're not just speaking me about the girls! Providing characters within the form of mini-figures and dolls lets in kids to increase their social play. It encourages imagination and the expression and labeling of emotions.

Blocks, Jigsaws, And Shape Sorters

Playing with blocks, jigsaws, and form sorters all lay the foundations of spatial thinking, logical reasoning, ordering, and recognizing various structures, ranges, and shading.

Play Dough

Play dough has a tremendous capacity for gaining knowledge. No longer best does it strengthen hands in practice for an entire life of writing; it teaches fine motor abilities, creativity, and hand-eye coordination. Upload a few beads to the dough for a pleasant-motor exercise, or get the kids threading beads on to lengths of dried spaghetti held within the dough, for extra play-fee.

Sand

Sand play is an exceptional possibility for the rules of clinical gaining knowledge of, and growing self-self belief and bodily development. Scooping, digging, pouring and sifting, train kids how things work, while additionally building their muscle tissue and coordination. Accomplished alongside a little pal, and it turns into approximately teamwork, sharing, and social talents.

Music, Dancing, And Singing

Singing and song highly assist to broaden language and shape the premise of literacy abilities, in addition to fundamental mathematical ideas consisting of counting. Moreover, they begin to expand rhythm, while additionally refining their listening talents. Dancing allows the kid to expand strength and coordination, and versatility.

Imaginative Play

All play must be imaginative, but we're relating to the kind of play that comes certainly too many kids. Go away a small toddler with nothing however a random choice of items and you'll quickly find them lost in a global of make-believe. Giving baby time and space for innovative play is vital. It develops their imagination, which is essential for literacy abilities and highbrow reasoning. Moreover, it increases their experience of self, and shallowness, as well as making feel of the sector around them, as well as the ability to address boredom.

To Ride, To Crawl, To Ascend, To Swing

Younger children are motivated to achieve something. Allowing them to achieve this, and presenting safe and age-suitable challenges lets in them to boom their confidence as well as expand their resilience via risk-taking. Of route, gross motor capabilities also acquire a mighty improve.

Nature Play

Kids' gaining knowledge of is fuelled with rocket-gasoline whilst you take the play area out into the tremendous outdoors. That's why wooded area colleges are so famous and especially appeared. Not simplest is it healthful, it teaches a recognize for the surroundings, and the beginnings of biology. It also allows kids to grow to be greater unbiased and inquisitive.

Sensory Play

In a nutshell, sensory play is any play hobby that involves contact, odor, flavor, sight and listening to. This can be provided with a plate of jelly, aqua beads, ice, rainbow rice, or even small global tubs. Sensory play stimulates exploration and the building blocks of technology and research.

Basic Board Games

There are such a lot of board games to be had for even the youngest gamers, and those should be embraced – no longer most effective for their laugh element, however for their learning capacity. In addition to the topics of numbers, hues, shapes, and early phonics, these games are vital for coaching kids flip-taking and sharing.

Drawing And Painting

Letting kids run wild with paints and drawing gear allows them to enjoy their world in a sensory way and develop self-expression, even as additionally growing pre-writing abilities. Moreover, it's an invitation to learn about hues, mixing, and precise-old tidying up

Cooking And Pretend-Cooking

Cooking and fake cooking, serving, and stores are superb play scenarios for children. Cooking itself combines factors of sensory play, mathematical principles, domestic safety, and following procedures. Faux cooking, serving, and toy shops additionally educate fundamental mathematical thoughts in addition to social interaction, and a way to be thoughtful to others.

The Cardboard Box

Sure sincerely! The humble cardboard container is one of the most super invites to play. Will, it's a residence, a vehicle, a domestic for his or her buddies? Offer them with scraps of fabric, cushions, pencils and paper plates and watch them discover their international, enter their imagination, and begin questioning like an engineer.

Chapter 9: Dealing With Difficult Toddlers

We have established that toddlers can be difficult, and the need to train them comes in. We should not just claim that they would understand when they are grown, no. it may be too hard for you to stop it when they are grown. They are toddlers, they are not dumb, and they know the difference between right and wrong. Remember the introduction, we are getting to the core of this book and I would want you to read this with an open mind. All am saying here, may not go well with your thinking but an open mind would make you think from different angles.

Four Common Struggles Toddlers May Have

To begin, we need to understand why toddlers could be difficult. For the first time, they are realizing that they are separate individuals from their parents and/or caregivers. The initial thought of an infant is that he/she is part of the parent but when they reach the toddler stage they realize that this isn't true. This also means that they become driven to assert themselves to communicate their likes and dislikes as well as trying to act independently. They are also trying to develop the language skills which will help them express their wants, ideas or needs.

Furthermore, toddlers do not understand the logic of waiting and the logic behind having everything. They no nothing or little about self-control and in a nut shell, he/she may be having a hard time balancing his/her needs with what you are providing as a parent or care giver. Toddlers could be difficult, they could be funny to. Here are four common situations your child could be struggling with:

He says no when he means yes. These happens when you are offering him a favorite treat.

He has a meltdown anytime you fail to understand his words.

He doesn't want any substitute. The blue pajamas or nothing else, even though they may not be washed or even after offering him the purple one.

He acts out when frustrated. Gives up everything when angry.

What is listed above are only acts which toddlers put on to manage strong feelings, since they are new to almost everything, they lack good control over what controls them and how they can control it. They are toddlers, they soon find out that they have vocal powers and that is when the crying, shouting and yelling increases. They may also want to try to make different noises to see how they sound and the reactions of adults around them to such noise. They impulsively go into an activity without much or any thinking. It is important for you to know that there exist a peculiarity in each child. They react differently to different situations, in fact you can even place a tag around them. Most times you can start with some funny names like bubbly, daredevil, determined, stubborn, cautious, adventurous etc. It may interest you to know that some challenging toddler behavior is developmentally correct, they may be defiant, bossy, sassy or impulsive but they are just byproduct of what the child needs-independence.

Eleven Difficult Behaviors and their Practical Solutions

Unfortunately, some bad behaviors are common among toddlers. Here are the eleven difficult behaviors and their practical solutions:

Aggression, hitting and biting

Interrupting

Lying

Pulling hair

Running away

Screaming

Tattling

Teasing

Throwing tantrums

Throwing things

Whining

Aggression, Hitting And Biting

Aggressive behavior is normal for toddlers, don't be surprised I said so. Now, I would provide you with practical solutions on what you are to do when you come across an aggressive toddler.

Make sure you keep your cool: keeping your cool shows how controlled you are, don't yell at the child when he/she is in the aggressive mode. If you tell your child she is bad, you are just getting her riled up.

Let's your limits be clear: Your reply to your aggressive toddler should be immediate. Make sure he/she is out of the situation for a brief time-out. Maybe a minute or two should give him/her time to cool down. Thereafter, you connect to the child after he/she has understood the consequences of the reaction.

Strengthen good behavior: I have mentioned this point behavior and would still say it again. Make sure you reward good behavior immediately you see it. You should not give your child attention only when he is misbehaving, catch him doing something good and praise him for it. An offer to push his swing or play together should be a reward for good behavior.

Provide logical consequences: If your child begins to throw Lego toys at other children while they are playing, take him or her away immediately and watch others play. During that process, explain that he/she can go back when she is ready to have fun without hurting other children.

Don't lecture or try to think like a toddler. You can't reason with them for now because they don't really understand the consequences of their actions.

Make discipline to be consistent: Children enjoy rote learning and with that, bits of information remain where there are stored. Make sure you respond to each episode of aggression the same way, so much you become predictable. This forms a pattern that the child recognizes and tries to avoid. This will eventually sink into their consciousness.

Alternatives should be taught: Explain to him or her briefly on the consequences of his or her last action. It is natural to have angry feelings but it is not okay to show them by kicking, hitting, or biting. He should apologize after lashing out someone for any reason. Such an apology should be sincere even though it may look insincere to you. With these, the lesson will sink in.

Keep your toddler active: If you notice your child is a high spirited one, give her plenty of unstructured time, make them outdoors preferably. This gives him much time to burn off abundance of energy.

Watch it: When it comes to screen time, as a parent you should watch whatever your child is watching. Not all cartoons are meant for children. Be mindful of the digital games and other media designed for young children. Several studies suggest that extreme screen time contributes to the bad behavior of a child and causes much problem as they grow. It may interest you to know that The American Academy of Pediatrics advises against TV and other screen which includes phones, computers and tablets until children are at least 18 months old. Even if your child is 18 months old, you should limit his screen time to not more than an hour a day. Choose what she is watching, and choose high-quality, age-appropriate media. A war movie with a lot of battle scenes wouldn't be good for an aggressive child. It would only upgrade his level of aggressiveness into something bloody or extreme.

Get help if you need help: Speak to a child doctor if you notice that your child's aggression is too much. But this should be when you have noticed some or all of the following features:

☐ Your child finds it easy to attack adults.

☐ He or she enjoys making other children upset or frightened

☐ He or she remains aggressive for more than a few weeks after you have tried all you could.

Interrupting

Nothing can be so exasperating than a child who obviously break in every time you are chatting with a friend. Toddlers don't really interrupt with words all the time but their actions. And that is because they always seek attention from their parents and may be jealous if a friend or an adult is getting all of it. In this aspect, it is your fault. You can do the following:

Chose the right locale for your meetings. A place where your child can play while you talk with the adult. A park having a sandbox is something nice.

Get a baby sitter. This would help a lot and would allow you use all focus or concentration during the meeting. Knowing that your child is in safe hands.

Teach your children polite behavior. A good way to teach them is by reading them some books like The Berenstain Bears Forget Their Manners, by Stan and Jan Berenstain or The Bad Good Manners Book, by Babette Cole's Aliki's Manners and What Do you Say, Dear? By Sesyle Joslin. Any book on good manners you can lay your hands on. Read it to them every day.

Schedule your phone calls. You wouldn't want your child to disturb you while you are on a call, so make necessary preparations.

Lying

First, why do children lie? They have active imagination and they are very forgetful. These cute angels may also have what we call angel syndrome. A child who thinks that his parents believe he can do know wrong would do wrong on purpose. When asked, a lie comes to mind. Toddlers do lie, and it is natural for them to do so. How can you stop this?

Always encourage truth-telling. You should not be mad at your child when he or she tells you the truth instead you should be happy. Show your child that honesty pays off.

You should not accuse your child for any reason. Your comments, remarks should help your child not put him down.

Don't weigh your child down with too many expectations. He or she would not understand. They are children, toddlers not adults. You shouldn't be expecting too much from them.

Build your trust. Assure your child that you trust him or her and don't puncture that trust.

Pulling Hair

To begin with, pulling hair, biting, pinching, hitting etc. are ways your child showcases his feelings or applies control over what seems to be his immediate environment (his body). Roberts, a professor of clinical psychology at Idaho State University in Pocatello claims that "a child might be pulling hair to make bad things go away." For whatever reason, you should take the following steps when these happens:

Let him or her know that it doesn't work. Demonstrating convincingly that an aggressive action would get your child nowhere is a key to suppressing aggression. Don't ignore it, demonstrate the futility of pulling hair and make sure he understands it.

Stop the behavior as soon as it starts. When you catch him holding a fistful of hair, stop him immediately. Hold his hand firmly while you keep repeating this sentence "we don't pull hair. Pulling hair hurts."

Take your time to give a detailed explanation, but make sure it is very brief. You start by asking him or her "what did you do that was wrong?" after the reply, you make use of that opportunity to tell him that pulling his hair only hurts himself and others.

You should not be guilty of the same offense. Don't pull your child's hair if you don't want them to pull it also.

Running Away

A running away toddler could be very funny. Like really? Where do they think they are going? But you have to be careful when this happens outdoors, especially on the walkway. Why do they run? Just like any other attitude displayed by a toddler, running away comes from a new sense of independence and the fact that he has legs that can run. Patricia Shimm, director of the Barnard College Center for Toddler Development in New York and co-author of Parenting Your Toddler says "toddlers love the feeling of being free and running around, you can encourage it as long as you can control where they run." You can't stop this, you can only control it:

Stay close to them and it should be okay for you to look ahead, when they are running.

Show him where he can run and where he can't. Allow him to explore the safe areas

Entertain your child.

Screaming

There are many reasons why toddlers scream. Most of the time, toddlers scream to get attention or demand for something. And we all know that a toddler's scream is very annoying. Screaming can be very embarrassing and when the toddler's volume is turned way up, it only aggravates you. You can do the following to curb this act:

You might want to run errands on your child schedule. Isn't the he dictating what he wants here? Oh yes he is and he has a right to do so. To save your eardrums, do the right thing at the right time.

You might want to stick to noisy restaurants when out. This only covers your secret and it becomes less embarrassing.

Encourage your child to make use of indoor voice. A simple shuu… while you place your finger on your lips is enough gesticulation for him or her to understand you.

Make shouting a game. This may sound ridiculous but once in a while, play a shouting game with your child. Indulge his need to be loud by saying, "Let's both yell as loud as we can," join him and after some seconds, make him stop by saying "Now, let's see who can whisper best"

Keep your child occupied.

Don't yell at your child. They imitate you, and it wouldn't take long for them to catch the screaming feeling.

Tattling

Why do children tattle? According to Jerry Wyckoff, a child psychologist in Prairie village, Kansas. "Tattling allow a child to one-up another child, to gain favor in the eyes of her parent or teacher." Some of the time, kids tattle because they have not developed the social or emotional skills required to solve skills all by themselves. Tattling has a positive effect too and it means that your child is showing you that he/she understands the rules and knows right from wrong. Before we go too far, what is tattling? It just simply means telling somebody, especially somebody in authority about something bad or the wrong doing of somebody else. Do you get report from your child about everything? “Mom, Michael is playing in that person’s car, Dad, Sarah is keeping a crayon in her pocket, Mom, Brian is playing with a sharp object . . . etc.” That’s tattling. The following steps can be taken:

Assess the situation: “it is hard for kids this age (toddler age) to make independent judgments about what’s tattle-worthy and what isn’t” Wyckoff said. Before you conclude that your child is a whiny tattletale, take a stock of the situation.

Put the work back on his shoulder for tattling. When your child understands that tattling only gets him more responsibility, he tends to mind his own business.

Teasing

You may agree or not, teasing is just what life brings. It happens when it happens and even toddlers are not left out of it. It is really painful when toddlers are teased and you should understand that as a parents. What can you do when a toddler is teased? This may not work well for toddlers as they would require verbal response.

Your child should not respond. This could be hard but it is a trick which can repel those guilty of the teasing offense.

You can coach your child to “agree” with what the teaser is saying. He/she would look dumb when a child says “I agree I suck my thumb”

Ask for help. Your child can ask for help from anyone or any adult around.

Throwing Tantrums

Of all the bad behaviors toddlers display, throwing tantrums seems to be the worse of them all. A temper tantrum can be equivalent to a summer storm. Something fierce and sudden. One minute, you and your child are in the middle of a perfect dinner, another he is whining and whimpering. As if that is not enough, she begins to scream at the top of her lungs.

Kids of ages 1 to 3 are prone to this. Quickly, I would provide seven tips on how to handle a tantrum:

First rule is that you don't lose your cool. There is nothing pretty about tantrum. In fact a child may add kicking, screaming pounding on the floor, holding his breath to the point of turning blue, etc. I know, this is very hard to handle, but he rest assured that when a child is having a tantrum, he or she is just trying to withhold his actual behavior. Don't lose yourself by getting overly frustrated. It may interest you to know that some experts suggest that you should calmly leave the room for a few minutes and return after your child has stopped crying but in this process, you should keep watch of the child. While some may recommend that you pick the child and hold him or embrace her some may disagree that what you have just done is just to encourage the child. You may want to employ the traditional try and error thing. Keep your calm and see what works best for your child.

Always remember that you are an adult not a kid. I noticed a child in a child care once. When he was having his tantrums, the child care giver was presenting him with a lot of things, he kept throwing them at her. No matter how long a tantrum might continue, you should not provide anything for the child. Tantrums should not be the good way for him to express his feeling.

Make use of a time-out occasionally. This depends on the age of the child. A time out could help him or her realize what must have gone wrong. Explain briefly, and give out punishment. I know you may be surprised when I say punishment, yes! Punishment. They need to be punished for misbehaving. Here comes another question, how do I punish a child of 18 months?

Once you have noticed any situation that may be prone to tantrums, you stay away from it. If you notice that he falls apart when he is hungry, a snack pack with you is no crime. If trouble exist when he or she wants to make transition from one activity to the next, you should be ready to give heads-up before the change occurs. Toddlers love to get the independent feeling, so they always prefer one thing from the other. They love to make choices, monitor how often you say no to their choices and how often they also say no to yours.

Show love to your child. Letting your child know that you love him after any tantrum could have two contrasting causes. One, a quick hug and telling him that you love him could silence him or otherwise. As a parent, you should show love to your child every time. Make them feel proud to have you as a parent not only when tantrums happen.

Even though daily tantrums are perfect normal part of the mid-toddler years, keeping an eye out for possible problems is very important. When having an extremely busy schedule could cause parental tension. All these can provoke tantrums.

Throwing Things

Throwing things is an enjoyable skill for many children between 18 months to 3 years. Naturally they just love throwing things and has nature would have it, it just take some fine simple, motor skills to open the fingers and let go of an object to any possible direction. Throwing things is fun for the toddlers. You are always mad when spaghetti winds up all over your just mopped kitchen floor but for a toddler, it is great fun and a perfect experience. What can you do about it? You really can't do anything about you just have to control it:

Show him what can be thrown. If she is encouraged to throw, she wouldlearn what not to throw. When you provide a lot of thing to throw like balls, etc. she would understand that there are somethings which can be throne and some other things which are meant to be kept. Playing throwing games can be very beneficial too.

Don't encourage aggressive throwing. Pull him out from playing when he shows signs of aggressive throwing which may hurt anyone. The key is to be brief, smart and disciplined. Whenever he gets angry.

Make clean up fun. Clean up with your child. Tell him to pick up everything he must have thrown. It may been an overwhelming task for a child's age, yes! But you wouldn't allow him to do much. Just make him know that throwing things is no good.

Make sure you use toddler-proof dishes. You should not make use of fine china or even breakable stoneware. This is safety and you should understand this.

Whining

Whining is natural to toddlers because they rely on adult for almost everything. How can a child get your attention so as to obtain what he needs? Whining of course. A child whines when he feels powerless and he has a pressing need. What can you do to stop it?

Define what you mean by whining. Some experts suggest that you can record your child, both in mid-whine and during normal conversation and when both of you are good, you can play it back and discuss about it. Point out whining, let him understand what it means.

Understand that your child needs attention and give it to her. Whenever your child request for something in a pleasant way, make sure you respond immediately. Even if you cannot answer his request, acknowledge the request and give him a short estimate of time. Be realistic, don't promise what you can't achieve.

Chapter 10: The Role Of Communication

Being able to effectively communicate with your child means that you are able to understand their calls for different needs and responding to those calls with an appropriate response. Doing this begins right from the age of infancy. It is nothing new for a parent to recognize, acknowledge, and answer these calls right from the time of birth. Babies cry and whine along with giving any number of cues to a parent for their many needs, from hunger or sleep to discomfort or needing to be held. Most parents are adept at recognizing these signs and responding to them appropriately. Even before the child is able to talk, they try and communicate with the help of cues. Cues such as pointing to a certain object when they need something, a bottle of juice perhaps, or holding up their hands when they need to be held, are common with kids who are yet unable to talk. It is important that a parent or caregiver acknowledges these cues and responds accordingly.

Using Appropriate Nomenclature

It is important that parents and kids resort to using proper names for their day-to-day used objects. Making a habit of using proper names for items regularly used goes a long way in ensuring that your child learns them quickly and this makes for swifter communications. Using correct names for everyday items encourages a child to learn them faster and use them correctly.

Avoid Baby Talk

The child might not yet know how to pronounce a certain word and might begin calling it by their own equivalent that might have a similar sound or a combination of similar sounding letters. For example, a child who wishes to say 'juice,' might instead say 'ja-ju.' This is fine, and while the child will learn to say juice over time, you can help them learn faster by saying 'juice' yourself and avoiding using 'ja-ju' for juice yourself. When parents use baby talk for different things to communicate with the child, it delays the learning curve of the child. Always try and use the proper names for objects and encourage your child to learn this way.

Respecting Your Child

Begin respecting your child early on. Even when they are young and unable to talk and communicate using words, make it a point to give them importance in interactions and include them whenever possible.

For example, if you are feeding your child, you could include them in the activity by saying something like, “Would you like to hold this spoon while mommy feeds you?”

Or if you are giving your child a bath and you recite rhymes while doing so as a bath-time-play, you could ask your child what rhyme they wish for and you could both sing that together. The point here is to make the child feel valued, included and respected. We want them to understand and believe that their choices and opinions matter to us and we are ready to hear them out. It is essential that you begin to inculcate this feeling as early as you can. Being valued and validated goes a long way in incorporating confidence in kids from an early age.

Expressing Emotions

Kids being able to express their emotions efficiently is an important part of having effective communication. But to do this, they would need our loving guidance to show them what it is that they are feeling. A parent can help their child in this regard by helping them name the emotion they are feeling.

For example, if you notice your child sitting quietly after they have just waved goodbye to their grandparents, you could say something like, “I understand you must be sad because grandma left for her trip. Are you missing her already? It’s ok to be sad.” Or something like, “You are pounding the table, you must be angry.”

What this practice does is that gives a name to what they are going through or the feeling they are experiencing. This is extremely helpful when you would like to teach them how to react or behave when they experience a similar feeling again in the future.

For example, you wish to tell your child that they ought to look at positive or brighter things when they are sad. But to do this, they would have to know what being sad is in the first place. Like when their grandma has gone for the trip, you would want them to look at the brighter side of things with something like, "You can make a welcome back card for her when she comes back." Or when your child is angry, you might want to say, "Take a deep breath three times when you are angry." Only when your child is able to relate the name of the emotion to what they felt when they experienced it themselves will they be able to grasp and put your advice into practice.

Naming emotions is also essential when you want to teach your child which emotions are fine to express, and which should be controlled.

Positive Talk

Another important pillar to excellent communication with kids, especially in the toddler age, is to use positive talk. This is when what you say consists of what the child can, should or must do instead of what they can't, shouldn't, or mustn't do.

Avoiding Negatives

Make it a habit to talk to your child in positive sentences. When you know that what you are going to say will involve a negation or denial of some kind, use a positive alternative to it in its place. A straight out 'no' is more difficult for a toddler to process than a positive alternative. Consider the following dialog between a toddler and a parent:

Child: Can we go to the park today?

Parent: No, not today.

Child: Why not today? I want to go now! I am bored.

Parent: I told you not today. Go play with your toys now.

This scenario can quickly escalate into a tantrum or even a meltdown. Now see the same dialog without the negatives.

Child: Can we go to the park today?

Parent: I think we'll go to the park tomorrow.

Child: But I am bored now!

Parent: How about we both play with your toys now and we go to the park tomorrow?

You see that the child refrains from asking, "Why not today?" in the second scenario because the parent hasn't really said, "Not today." Instead, they used a positive alternative. Also, it is important to notice that the parent has involved the child to validate their reasoning and choice of activity, along with offering to play with them instead of themselves. It is an important approach to be mindful of.

Using 'no' frequently to answer your child's requests and wishes can turn them bitter from within. It generates a feeling of being denied time and again when faced with an outright no. Instead, if the same is relayed using a positive alternative, it doesn't have the same drastic effects and is more encouraging and confidence-building for the child.

Reframing

Also important is to avoid a constant barrage of negative instructions. If a child is used to hearing things like, 'don't do this, don't do that,' on a regular basis, this can only sow resentment in the child's mind toward the parent. And that is not something a parent would ever want. See the following example to understand the scenario better.

If your child is running around in the house or jumping on the sofa, you are bound to say something like "don't run" and "don't jump." Instead, you could simply reframe the sentences to avoid the negative and say something like, "We should walk inside the house. You may run when outside in the garden or the park," and "We jump on the ground and sit on the sofa."

You could even attach a line of caution with respect to values you follow at home or about their own safety that might be at stake due to their actions. But never begin your instruction or advice with a negative. Give up using 'don't' in such situations.

Doing this ensures your child doesn't feel restricted or denied simple pleasures constantly.

Practical Strategies for Effective Communication

There are a few actionable points that you can make use of and put into practice when you wish to communicate with your child with ease and efficiency. Keeping these tips in mind will help you talk in a manner that your child can easily understand and, at the same time, accept what you are saying for the value it carries. You will be able to reach your child more effectively this way.

Maintaining Eye Level

Always make it a point to talk to your kids when you are at their level. Get down, either on your knees or with your back bent, so you are on the same level with your child. Being on the same level as them is similar to taking them into confidence before saying anything. This simple step makes you more approachable and easier to understand. Even if what you are saying is not of an intimidating nature, your straight and unyielding stance can make it appear to be so. Therefore, it is always a good idea to talk to kids when at their same level. Also, when they are talking, and you are simply listening, being on their level shows interest on your part, and your child would, therefore, be more willing to talk and open up to you this way.

Affirm and Repeat

When your child is trying to tell you something, either through words, fully framed sentences, or just gestures and cues, it is always advisable to affirm their thoughts out loud. Repeat after them to let them know you are listening to them and are ready to hear them out and understand their needs or wishes. This is especially true in the case of younger kids of around two years who have just begun to talk. This can also help you understand them better when all you have are a few broken words or gestures to go on. Affirming their opinions and repeating after them gives them a chance to acknowledge if what you have understood is indeed what they have been trying to say or deny and alter their approach to help you understand better.

For example, "You are pointing at that teddy, do you wish to play?" or

“I understand you want to have ice cream but let’s have it together after dinner.”

Parental Narratives

Narratives are when you involve your child in your day to day activities by talking to them about the work you are doing, or telling them a story of your past or some hilarious anecdote from your childhood. The point here is to talk to them and make them feel involved. These simple narrations can help establish an atmosphere of ease around your child and help them be confident about opening up to you in a similar way when they need to. It also gives them a sense of importance to know that you think them important enough to share such things with them, and they will be more willing to reciprocate in the future.

For example, if you are making an omelet and your child is sitting at a table near you, just talk to them about what you are doing in a simple narrative. Or you could talk to them about an omelet related story from your childhood. Making them feel involved and valued is the key.

Chapter 11: The Key To Cooperation

Affection and care

By giving your toddler the greatest affection and care, you encourage him to be well-adjusted and well-behaved. It is crucial that your toddler understands how to trust you, and this is because he knows you are there to fulfill his needs. This trust means that your early age toddler will feel safer and less anxious in the long run. He will have faith in you when it is time to create limits and laws, and he will realize that even though you correct him, you love him.

Real-life example: Your 12-month-old kid loves playing with you, but may get upset or angry when the time comes for you to go out. It is essential to let your baby know that he/she needs to stay calm, even if he/she is upset. You need to control your toddler frustration and also need to handle your feelings, so with this strategy, the toddler will learn to trust you and learn that even when he/she is in trouble, the world is safe. And, of course, there will be plenty of game possibilities later.

Consistent

It is essential to be consistent when it comes to discipline. Parents who do not obey the rules and consequences they have developed they often fail to train their toddlers. For instance, if you tell your kid that timeout is the effect in response to the bad behavior, make sure you follow it. Empty threats weaken your power. And don't forget that children learn to watch adults, especially their parents. Make sure your own action is a role model. When you ask your child to gather toys, you will feel much better if you have put your own things away than left your things all around the house.

Fight with Anger

Toddlers of 1-2 years of age sometimes fight with great feelings of frustration and rage. Their social and emotional skills are only beginning to grow. By listening to its emotions, adjusting the environment, distracting, and preparing for tough circumstances, you will help your toddler to do well.

Remain calm

When your toddler heads for an inappropriate or dangerous play object, say calmly "No" and either remove your kid from the field or distract him or her with another activity. You mustn't spank your kid, hit, or slap. It is doubtful that children will equate actions with physical punishment at this age. The message you give when you spank is that when you're mad, it's all right to hit someone. Researchers claim that spanking is no more effective than other practices like timeouts.

Speak the language of your kid

If your kid is upset, it is best to keep contact very simple. Using short phrases with lots of repetition, motions, and facial expressions to show your child what is happening in his mind. Saying "I can see you are upset" to your child not only shows him that you seek to understand but also extends his emotional vocabulary.

Example: Your child yanks a toy truck from the hands of his friend. Give the toy to the other child instead of giving it a timeout or attempting to justify why it was incorrect. Try to ecologically echo what your child appears to think of and feel back to him: "I know you want the truck." If you validate your child's feelings, it may help him settle down. Give him the simple version again: "No grabbing, no grab, this is max's turn." It may at first feel stupid, but it's going to work!

Don't Use No word to avoid

"No" is one of the first phrases that many toddlers learn to use, and it almost inevitably is the one they use most frequently. As a parent, this is important; you take the word "No" seriously to avoid these repetitive "No" when your child says it.

Example in real life: You gave your little baby lunch, but he didn't eat the banana you picked up for him. Ask if he/she wants to eat it, and take the banana away if he/she says no. You can still try to give the banana later. But if you listen to the refusal of your baby, he/she will learn that the word "No" can carry some weight. Although, if you take the banana away, the toddler will realize something is not working, and this will stop him from immediately saying it.

Replace and restore

Unlike us all, young children learn by doing. So, when your child does something you don't like, you don't have to stand by. And you don't want to stand by if your little one reaches for dangerous things. Take the object away or push your kid physically. Then offer him a healthy option as a replacement. Make sure you explain, even if he's too young to really understand what you're doing to your toddler. An important lesson you teach him is that such conduct is not acceptable. Example of real life: Your 12-month-old finds your jewelry box and plays with it. Your toddler loves it because it's colorful, and you saw him wearing your necklace. Rather than let him keep it, take away your necklace and say that your jewelry box is not a toy. Then give your child a few colorful toys and say, "They're okay to play with."

Correct attention action

Around some point, probably about the first birthday of your toddler, he/she will begin to understand how he can press the buttons for attention. There's a difference between dropping peas on the ground because they investigate his food and throwing them into the ground intentionally to respond. You know it is time to do something when he sees you in his eye and drops his meal. That's to show him that his actions have repercussions. Example of real life: Your toddler made a mess under his high chair. Once he's done feeding, pick it up, set it on the floor, and ask him to help you with your peas. Tell him what you're doing, "Look, the floor is messy, because you dropped peas, so you have to clean it."

Chapter 12: Taming Tantrums

All parents go through the battles of taming the tantrums of their toddlers. It is something inevitable during childhood, in particular between 1-4 years of age. One minute your child is happily playing, the next thing you know, he is thrashing and howling like a ball of rage. He kicks, shoves, cries, shrieks, lashes out, and even bites. The child does not even know that he is hurting others and does not display the slightest remorse afterward. The reason is that the temper display is beyond his understanding, and he only acts out to express his fury or frustration over something he desires at the moment.

Understanding What Leads to Fits of Rage

There are many reasons why toddlers have tantrums. Basically, it is his way of communicating with you or with people around him. He does not have a command of the language yet, so your child uses his body to demand attention, fulfill his needs, or cope up with the challenges that come his way.

The Common Causes of Tantrums Are:

- Hunger, fatigue, sickness, boredom, overstimulation, or physical discomfort

Any of them can cause the toddler to throw a fit. The tantrum is his cry for help or saying "enough". Since he does not know how to express it, he resorts to what he can do- whining, screaming, lying on the floor with arms flailing, throwing things, and more frustrating acts. There are cases when tantrums are caused by physical problems, which include prolonged digestive problems and painful acid reflux, so be watchful.

- Frustration

Frustration triggers the child's anger, resulting in temper tantrums. Toddlers are naturally active and want to test or do everything that he sees others are doing. However, because he is still uncoordinated or weak, it frustrates him. Since he cannot control his temper, he acts out, shows aggression, or displays antisocial behavior.

- Desire for attention

Young children crave a lot of attention, and they will do everything to the extent of facing the consequences rather than be ignored by their parents.

- Need to be independent

Small as they are, toddlers can test the patience of parents by doing what they want to do. The tantrum is their way of asserting independence and gain control over the immediate environment, leading to power struggles between them and their parents. Upon discovering that there are boundaries and restrictions, they resort to tantrums to show defiance.

- Not getting what he wishes.

Toddlers do not have strong control over their impulses and desires; expecting adults around them will give what they want. It is the reason why your child has a hard time managing his disappointment when you deny his demand. He does not understand why you say "no" or "later." He wants it now and does not comprehend the concept of delayed gratification.

- Changes

Small or big changes and transitions upset toddlers. Anything that affects his scheduled activities or routine will make him overwhelmed or emotionally lost.

- Testing

The toddler stage is the start of the child's awareness of the power he can wield over others. He constantly tests the limits and boundaries, experimenting with the behavior that will help him get what he wants.

- Curiosity

He is trying to learn things about the world around him and curious about the sounds and sight. Sometimes, due to his curiosity, he does things that are beyond acceptable behavior and can compromise his safety. Do not be surprised when he pulls the tail of the cat or bangs the table or uses crayons to doodle on the wall.

Other significant facts about tantrums:

- It is a normal toddler behavior.

- Beware of extreme tantrum that includes destruction, aggression, occurs up to 5-10 times daily, or last for more than 10 minutes. It may indicate an underlying issue that requires professional help.

- It is most common when the child is between the ages of 2 and 3.

- Sometimes, it is a symptom of inward-directed disorder like depression or anxiety, which is usually easy to disregard among active toddlers.

- It can be part of an outward-directed misbehavior pattern, causing the child to demonstrate excessive aggression, which includes destroying things or harming himself and other people. If this is the case, he may be experiencing symptoms of attention deficit hyperactivity disorder (ADHD).

Now that you know the various causes of tantrums, you can plan in advance and prevent (or reduce) its occurrence. One way to study the pattern of his tantrums is to keep a journal and take note when it happens, where it happens, what kind of behavior he displays, what triggers it, how does it end, and more.

Preventing Tantrums

There is no foolproof way to prevent tantrums because they are beyond the control of toddlers, but you can encourage good behavior with the following strategies:

- Plan ahead. Before going to fulfill outside errands, make sure that your child is not hungry and tired. When you expect to wait in line, bringing his favorite snack or toys to keep him occupied. Anticipating what can happen will set him up for success.

- Be consistent. Establishing a day-to-day routine teaches the child to know what you expect of him. Sticking to the routine is important, including his bedtime and naptime. Be sure to set simple and reasonable limits.

- Point out his good behavior. Hugging your child or praising him when he is behaving well boosts his self-esteem and looks forward to this extra attention. The more positive reinforcement he receives for the desired behavior, the more he will do it again.

- Allow the child to make his own choices. Avoid the habit of saying “no.” If you want him to gain a sense of independence and control, let him make choices on simple tasks like what color of shoes he wants to wear or the fruit he likes to eat. Let him choose the activity he wants to do and play with him regularly.

- Avoid situations that can trigger temper tantrums. Keep him away from areas that will trigger his desire to buy a sweet treat or toys if you are not buying him one. If he is easily bored, avoid taking him to restaurants that do not offer fast service. Do not give him toys that are too complex and advanced for his age or ability.

8 Ways to Handle Your Toddler's Temper Tantrums in Public

Every parent has been there- a child having an epic meltdown in public. What to do during this scenario?

Here are some ways to tame the tantrum:

Strategy #1 – Stay calm and ignore him.

Unless he physically endangers his safety or others, it is best to ignore him. Often, toddlers try screaming and crying to convince parents to give what they want. It is important not to lose your temper.

Strategy #2 – The louder he yells, the softer you talk.

Keep your composure and talk to your child in a calm, relaxed tone to soothe him. You can even try whispering in a gentle voice to gain his attention. This strategy usually works because the child is wondering what you are trying to say, making him quiet down to hear it.

Strategy #3 – Don't give in.

Giving in to your toddler's demand and letting him have his way is the worst idea. It will make the child think that acting out whenever he wants something is a means to an end. Stand your ground by repeating the rule.

For instance, you do not allow him to eat a cookie before dinner. If he insists on having one and displaying a tantrum, you can respond with "Cookies are not allowed before dinner" again and again in a neutral and calm voice. In due time, he will stop whining and understand that you mean business.

Strategy #4 – Avoid punishment in any form.

Remember that the tantrum display is just a phase that pretty soon will pass. It is important to be patient and avoid punishing him for throwing fits, no matter how irritating it is. Your toddler is learning how to cope up and interact. He still does not understand why he can't have everything he wants. Avoid spanking, yelling, and other punitive acts.

Strategy #5 – Empathize with the child.

A minor outburst is an indication that your child feels that he is not being understood or heard. It is best to catch it early and prevent the act from escalating into a full temper tantrum. A good strategy is to empathize with his feelings, letting the child know that you understand him and wishing you can allow or give him what he desires. Then, gently explain why you cannot. You can offer him a better option.

Strategy #6 – Get a breath of fresh air.

When your child seems inconsolable, take him outside to get a breath of fresh air. A change in the atmosphere helps to calm a crying kid.

Strategy #7 – Play a game and make him laugh.

Engage your toddler in a simple game like "I Spy" or "hide-and-seek," but make sure that he stays within eyesight, especially in a large public area. One example is to hide and pop quickly behind a rack of clothes, then reappear with a soft boo. When your child is enjoying and having fun, it keeps tantrums at bay.

Strategy #8 - Hold him close without saying a word.

When no amount of reasoning or ignoring does not stop him from crying, the best resort is to hug him. During this overwhelming act, your child does not hear or see you. You can only rely on the power of touch to soothe him and help him regain self-control. Picking up your toddler and hugging him gently and firmly will make him feel loved and understood. Sometimes, children want a safe place to calm their overwhelming feelings.

Keeping Your Toddler Safe during Tantrum Display

If he begins to start biting, kicking, throwing things, or hitting, then it is necessary to remove the child from the situation that triggers the meltdown. Pick your child firmly and hold him tightly to prevent hurting himself, avoid pulling or dragging. Find a private spot to calm him, allowing him to vent his bad moods. Giving him some space helps him manage his emotions, pulls himself together, and regains self-control.

After the Tantrum

The child is most vulnerable after the tantrum, so it is important to give him a hug to reassure him that he is still loved despite his acting out. Once he is completely calm, praise your toddler for regaining self-control like telling him, "I like how you calm down." Avoid giving what he wants after the storm. Make sure that he rests and gets some sleep to recover from the dramatic situation.

Chapter 13: How To Stop Toddler Temper Tantrums

Temper tantrums are common among toddlers. This is because toddlers have the cognitive skills to know what they want, but their communication skills make it difficult to express that. Additionally, toddlers don't have the coping skills to deal with negative emotions so throwing a tantrum is sometimes the most satisfying option for them. While tantrums can be frustrating, there are many things you can do to deal with these tantrums. Find ways to stop the tantrum, teach the toddler healthy ways to express their emotions, and understand why a toddler might throw a tantrum in the first place.

Stopping Your Toddler's Tantrum

Evaluate the situation. Take a few moments to consider the source of your child's tantrum before reacting. Do you know what they are angry about? Are they scared or injured? The reason a child is upset will dictate how you handle the tantrum.

In some situations, it's best to just let the toddler go through their tantrum without giving them too much attention. This is particularly true when you know your child is throwing a tantrum to try and manipulate you into giving them what they want. If you can see that your child is really losing it, it may be best to just leave them be.

If your child is crying because something frightened them or because they are very overwhelmed by a situation, you shouldn't ignore them. In this situation, they need your comfort to feel secure

Don't try to reason with an angry toddler. Trying to reason with a toddler in the midst of a major meltdown won't do any good. They are simply too caught up in their own emotions to listen to you, or understand what you are trying to say.

Their reaction may not make sense to you, but keep in mind that toddlers don't have the same reasoning and coping skills that you have as an adult. They are just reacting in a way that makes sense for them.

Understand that this doesn't mean you should just walk off and leave your child by themselves if it wouldn't be safe to do so. For example, you don't want to leave them sitting on the floor in the middle of a busy grocery store.

On the other hand, if you are in the safety of your home, you might let your child have their meltdown alone in their room. Giving them their space when it is safe to do so is a good way to give you both time to deal with your emotions without engaging in a battle.

Try to distract them. If you catch it before your child goes into total meltdown, distracting them may help avoid the problem altogether. If they are already throwing a tantrum, a distraction could help them calm down more quickly. Use something that you know they will be interested in. If you are going to go somewhere where a tantrum is likely, be sure to throw a few items for distraction into your bag before you leave home.

If there are signs that a tantrum is about to begin, pull out one of the items and say, "Look what I have here! Would you like to play with it?" If they nod, then hand it to them. If they shake their head, try a different item.

If your child is already having a tantrum, you can try the same thing, though it may be more difficult to get them to focus on what you are offering.

Small toys and healthy snacks are good items for distraction.

Do something silly. It isn't too hard to get a toddler to laugh. Try doing something silly to help your child focus on something other than their anger. Laughter also releases chemicals in the brain that help your child feel better about the situation.

For example, if you are at a store, hide for a few seconds behind something, then pop out with a big smile and say, “Boo!” You could also try making silly faces or talking in a funny voice.

Don’t give in. When your child is in the midst of a tantrum, the easiest thing to do will be to give in, especially if you are in a public place and feeling embarrassed. However, you should avoid giving in no matter how embarrassed or frustrated you feel. This is because giving in teaches your child that a tantrum gets them what they want, which means that the next time you tell them they can’t have something they want, they’ll use this technique again.

If you are feeling very embarrassed try leaving the situation before it gets worse. For example, if you are at the grocery store and your child throws a tantrum the second you walk in the door, you might consider putting off the shopping until later in the day. It may be frustrating, but it will be less frustrating than dealing with a cranky toddler throughout the shopping trip.

Control your temper. Parenting is a tough job, and sometimes the best thing you can do is just walk away if the situation permits. If you are feeling like you are about to lose your temper, remove yourself from the situation. If you are at home, let your child have their meltdown in a safe space, and go to another room where you can calm down for a few minutes. If you are in public, take your child to the car, put them in their seat, and spend a few minutes taking deep breaths outside the car while you calm down.

Many recommend taking slow, deep breaths while counting to ten in order to calm down.

Conclusion

The majority of parents don't wish to discipline their child, especially if they're just a toddler. I hate toddler discipline, but you only can't avoid it if your child is naughty; otherwise, how do they learn right from wrong?

When I was a toddler, I want to get a sound spanking once in a while. Still, now I realize that I deserved it, but in today's society, parents look to other sorts of toddler discipline to avoid having to offer physical punishment.

Even as a toddler in their very early stages of life, you ought to be setting a couple of basic rules from all the strategies I even have shared during this guide. Not too many, about 4 or 5, maybe a good figure.

One thing you should remember when setting these rules is that you got to be firm with them. If you set rules, you should stand by them; otherwise, there's not much point, inform your toddler what the principles are, then if they break one re-evaluate the rule, whenever they are doing so. Your toddler should also realize that you are simply the parent; they need to try what you say.

Of course, toddlers are well behaved also as sometimes naughty; once they are well behaved, then give your child praise, and this may reinforce to them that with good behavior, they get praised, but with bad behavior, they're going to get disciplined.

When your toddler misbehaves, then act with a firm, authoritative voice. If they're asked to show the TV off for instance and that they won't be firm once you say "Do as I say," don't say it with anger. If your toddler discipline isn't working and your

toddler is defiant, don't concede. If you concede, this is often a sure sign that they're going to act defiant next time and obtain their way.

Parents must be conscious of using positive words when they lecture their toddlers. Avoid using label words like bad, naughty, and other negative descriptions. Toddlers are often affected that psychologically, like resulting in low self-esteem rather than saying "stop" and "no," parents must say what exactly they need their toddlers to try to.

The words "Stop" and "no" are ineffective if used frequently. Save these words for grave instances, not together with your along with your"> together with your everyday conversations with your toddlers. Toddlers, same like adults, would likely listen if we tell them what to try to, not what we do not want them to try to.

CPSIA information can be obtained
at www.ICGtesting.com
Printed in the USA
BVHW041730060821
613849BV00017B/488

9 781989 965733